Cultivating Thinking in English and the Language Arts

Cultivating Thinking in English and the Language Arts

Robert J. Marzano
Mid-Continent Regional Educational Laboratory

National Council of Teachers of English
1111 Kenyon Road, Urbana, Illinois

Staff Editor: David A. Hamburg

Cover Design: Carlton Bruett

Interior Design: Tom Kovacs for TGK Design

NCTE Stock Number 09918-3020

This publication is based on work sponsored wholly, or in part, by the Office of Educational Research and Improvement, Department of Education, under Contract Number 400-86-0002. The content of this publication does not necessarily reflect the views of OERI or any other agency of the U.S. Government.

Library of Congress Cataloging-in-Publication Data

Marzano, Robert J.
Cultivating thinking in English and the language arts / Robert J. Marzano.
p. cm.
Includes bibliographical references (p.)
ISBN 0-8141-0991-8
1. English language—Study and teaching—United States. 2. Language arts—United States. 3. Thought and thinking—Study and teaching—United States. 4. Cognitive learning—United States.
I. Title
LB1576.M392 1991
428'.007—dc20 91-9493
CIP

Contents

1 A Framework for Cultivating Thinking

Recent years have seen a growing interest in teaching students how to think. Reports from the National Assessment of Educational Progress have warned that students across the nation do poorly on items that require higher-order thinking (Burns 1986), and calls for the teaching of thinking skills within the public schools have even been raised in Congressional hearings (Resnick 1987). The increasing concern over a lack of thinking skills has not gone unnoticed by the media either. In the spring of 1989, for instance, ABC news devoted a series, hosted by Barbara Walters, to the need for teaching thinking.

While the need for teaching thinking has been established, the best method is still a matter of debate. Some theorists assert that thinking should be taught in a pure, content-free environment. For example, Beyer (1988) believes that strategies and techniques for specific types of thinking should be introduced in a content-free manner and then applied to academic content. Similarly, de Bono (1985) has developed over sixty thinking strategies that are meant to be taught and practiced in isolation and then applied to academic areas. In sharp contrast, Resnick (1987) and Glaser (1984) state that thinking should be taught within the environment of content-area instruction. Glaser goes so far as to assert that there is no such construct as a generic thinking skill that can be practiced outside of a specific content area.

In this monograph somewhat of a middle position is taken, although it is biased toward the Resnick and Glaser end of the continuum. I do not take the position that thinking skills should be taught in isolation as generic processes, nor do I take the position that thinking skills are always domain specific. Rather, I assert that there are some generic types of thought that apply to all content; however, these types of thought are meaningful only when employed within specific content domains. Hence, this book presents ways of teaching and reinforcing, or cultivating, generic types of thought as applied to the teaching of English and the language arts.

A common and quite valid reaction to the suggestion that thinking should be taught and reinforced within any given content area is that thinking is already a part of all content-related learning. Although this is true, it does not negate the need for the teaching and reinforcement of thinking. Specifically, even though one quite naturally thinks and reasons when learning a given content, one does not necessarily also learn to think and reason better at the same time. For example, everyone breathes (thinks and reasons) quite naturally. Yet everyone can learn to breathe (think and reason) better.

Cultivating thinking within English and the language arts, then, is a matter of enhancing the natural cognitive processes involved in learning. From this perspective one can infer that a prerequisite for any instructional effort to enhance thinking is a firm understanding of some basic principles of learning.

Principles of Learning and Thinking

Although there are many theories of learning, each with its own distinctions, there are also a number of general themes or principles that seem to cut across all theories. Four general principles are described below:

Principle 1: Learning Occurs in a Mental Context

Learning of any type takes place in a mental environment that either enables or inhibits the learning process. A mental environment might be likened to a filter through which all perceptions pass, or the "context" in which learning occurs. Glasser (1981) and Powers (1973) explained that this context is composed of attitudes and beliefs, while Weiner (1972, 1983) noted that attitudes and beliefs are the stimuli for both affect and behavior.[1]

To say that beliefs affect behavior implies that success or failure in English and the language arts is a function of the beliefs students bring to class—specifically beliefs about English and the language arts. To illustrate, students in an American literature class will have beliefs about American literature that will affect their readiness to learn. If they believe that American literature is important and serves a valuable function in their lives, then they will bring a great deal of energy and enthusiasm to the class. However, if they do not perceive any value in American literature relative to their lives, then they will bring little energy to the learning situation.

Beliefs about the value of content, then, are a powerful aspect of the mental context in which someone learns. Beliefs about ability are another significant part of that context, for even if a student perceives

---

[1] Although there is a close relationship and fine distinction between beliefs and attitudes, these are not relevant to the discussion in this text. Hence, the terms *beliefs* and *attitudes* are used synonymously throughout.

content as valuable, little energy will be brought to the learning situation if the student believes that the skills necessary to master the content lie outside the scope of her abilities. Thus, if the American literature student perceives the content as important but beyond her abilities, she will bring little commitment to the learning situation. As Covington (1983) noted, the student might feign commitment in such situations, but will expend a minimum amount of energy.

The mental context in which students learn, then, is composed of an interactive system of beliefs and attitudes that affects students' commitment to and ultimate success at content-area learning. To teach thinking effectively requires a considerable amount of attention to this context.

Principle 2: Learning Involves the Construction of Meaning

Learning, especially during the initial stages of acquiring information, is fundamentally a constructive process. Specifically, Wittrock (1974) has shown that the learner acquires new knowledge by attaching what she already knows to what she is about to learn. Some theorists explain the construction of meaning in terms of schema activation. Schemata are packets of organized knowledge that help us make sense of the world around us (Rumelhart 1980). New information must be matched with existing schema so that it can be understood. To illustrate, consider the paragraph below:

> If the balloons popped the sound wouldn't be able to carry since everything would be too far away from the correct floor. A closed window would also prevent the sound from carrying, since most buildings tend to be well insulated. Since the whole operation depends upon a steady flow of electricity, a break in the middle of the wire would also cause problems. Of course, the fellow could shout but the human voice is not loud enough to carry that far. An additional problem is that a string could break on the instrument. Then there could be no accompaniment to the message. It is clear that the best situation would involve less distance. Then there would be fewer potential problems. With face to face contact, the least number of things could go wrong. (Bransford & Johnson 1972, 719)

Although the words and even entire sentences in this paragraph might make sense, it is difficult (if not impossible) to understand this passage—impossible, that is, until the appropriate schema is attached. To illustrate, consider the picture in figure 1.1.

Bransford and Johnson used this passage to illustrate that deriving meaning is not simply a matter of recognizing information as presented.

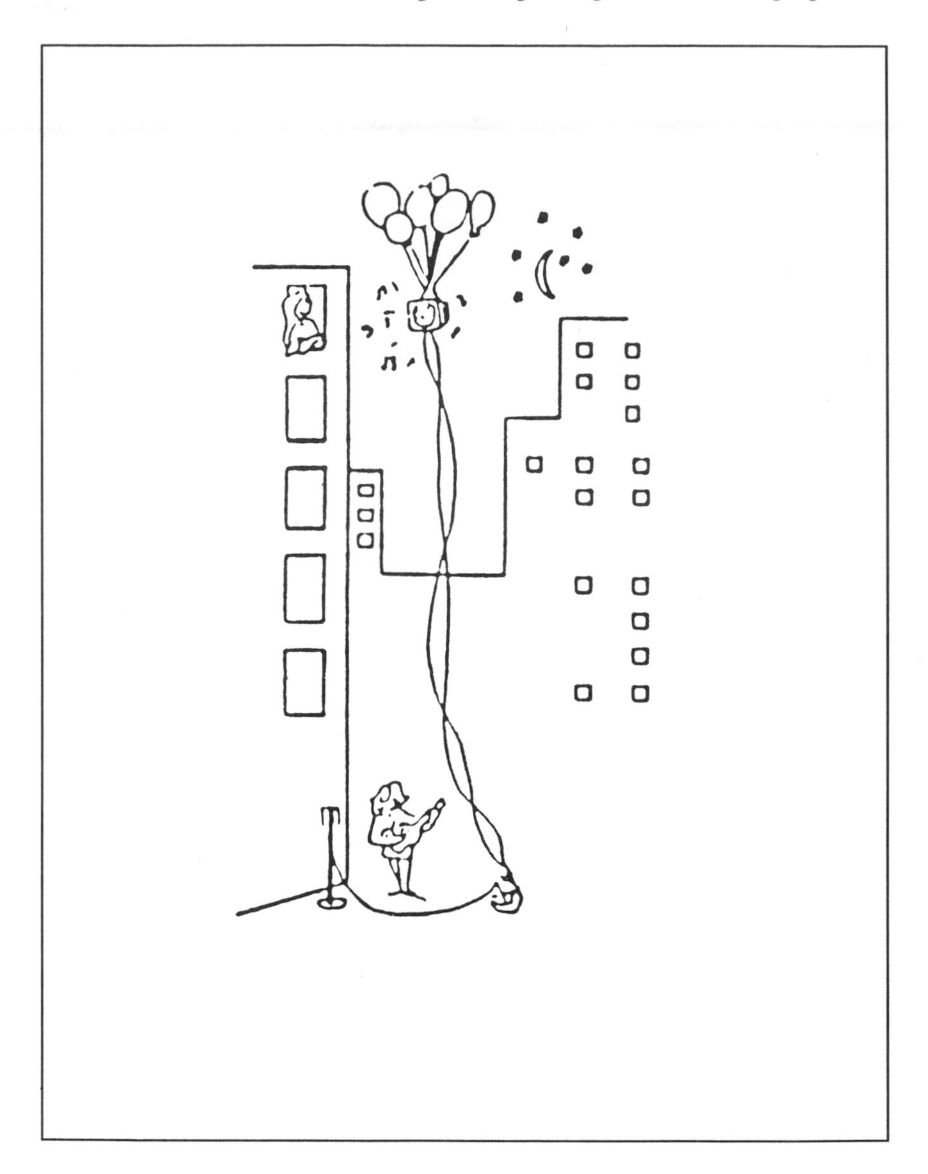

Fig. 1.1. Schema for Bransford and Johnson passage. From J. D. Bransford and M. K. Johnson, Contextual Prerequisites for Understanding: Some investigations of comprehension and recall. *Journal of Verbal Learning and Verbal Behavior 11*, pp. 717–726. Copyright 1972 by Academic Press. Reprinted by permission.

Rather, the learner first activates schemata appropriate to the information and then uses those schemata to interpret the information.

Relative to learning, such use of schemata indicates that in order to comprehend incoming information, the learner must initially "build his own meaning" by linking old information to new information. The process of linking also indicates that learning is a highly subjective act: The meaning constructed by one learner will invariably be somewhat different from that constructed by another, which, in the realm of English and the language arts, implies that students must be aware of the need to construct meaning and possess the tools to do so. This need is particularly evident in the area of the reader's response to literature.

Rosenblatt (1967) is commonly credited with articulating the importance and characteristics of literary response as a constructive process. Her remarks were in sharp contrast to the perspective of the New Criticism, which viewed response to literature as a highly analytic process in which meaning is discerned solely within the confines of the text. Since Rosenblatt's landmark critique there have been many discussions about the importance of the constructivist approach to literary response (Fish 1980; Probst 1988). Although some instructional implications of a constructive approach to literary response have been described (Probst 1988), current research and theory on cognition greatly enhance these efforts. For example, research in cognition indicates that response to narration is qualitatively different from response to exposition (Kintsch 1974; van Dijk 1980). This suggests that different strategies should be employed to facilitate students' responses to different types of content. Further, different types of response utilize different types of cognition. Thus, any attempt to teach thinking in English and the language arts should include activities that stimulate varied and distinct types of responses, and instruction should focus not only on students' capacities to respond, but on the different types of cognition that characterize different responses.

Principle 3: Once Acquired, Knowledge Undergoes Change

Knowledge once acquired through the construction of meaning is not static. Rather, it is developed and restructured in a number of ways, some of which are quite surprising and unpredictable (Vosniadou & Brewer 1987). There are a number of different descriptions of the structural changes that occur to information once it has been initially acquired.

Rumelhart and Norman (1981) assert that existing knowledge (schemata) can be modified in three ways: accretion, tuning, and restructuring. *Accretion* refers to the changes in knowledge over time due to the gradual accumulation of information; it involves additive components. *Tuning* refers to the creation of generalizations about existing schema and the identification of default values. Finally, *restructuring* refers to the creation of new structures either to reinterpret old information or to create new information. According to Rumelhart and Norman, then, changes in knowledge structures can be placed on a continuum that ranges from gradual, additive changes (accretion) to drastic reorganization (restructuring).

In a similar vein, Vosniadou and Brewer identify a number of categories of knowledge change, two of which concern us here: weak restructuring and strong restructuring. Weak restructuring involves the creation of new and more numerous links among information in long-term memory. It also involves the use of more abstract schemata to represent information. Strong, or radical, restructuring involves the development of totally new theories to explain and organize information. Where weak restructuring makes a knowledge base more complex and abstract, radical restructuring changes the theory base or explanatory system that guides the organization of information.

Common to all theories of knowledge change is the principle that the more drastic the change, the more complex the tasks the learner must engage in and the more time the learner must take to adapt to the new knowledge. In fact, Jacques (1985) noted that the level of knowledge change the learner experiences is directly proportional to the complexity of the tasks in which the learner involves himself and the length of time the learner engages in those tasks.

In the practice of instruction, this means that students must engage in complex tasks that extend far beyond the boundaries of a single class period—tasks that last a week, two weeks, a semester, or longer. One such task, composition, is already a staple of English and language arts instruction. As emphasized by recent research (Bereiter 1980; Bereiter & Scardamalia 1982; Flower & Hayes 1980a, 1980b, 1981), the composing process by definition is cognitively complex and requires an extended period of time to complete. A learner routinely changes and restructures his knowledge base relative to the topic about which he writes.

Current research in cognition illustrates that there are other such tasks that can radically restructure knowledge. For example, the process of scientific inquiry is highly complex and requires an extended period of time to complete. Invariably, the learner changes and restructures his knowledge relative to the topic to which he applies the process scientific inquiry. This implies that in addition to, or as a part of their efforts in composition, students in English and language arts should be engaged in scientific inquiry about language, literature, and drama as a complementary method for enlarging and developing their knowledge base.

Principle 4: Higher-Order Thinking Is Dispositional in Nature

It is a common misconception that higher-order thought is complex thought, that the more complex a task is, the higher the level of cognition required. Although it seems intuitively valid that the complexity of a task dictates whether it is higher or lower in order, the problem with this conception is that very complex tasks can be done with relatively little effort or thought. To illustrate, consider the cognitive complexity involved in reading this chapter. For years researchers and theorists have agreed that the act of reading is one of the most complex of cognitive operations, yet no literate adult would consider the act of reading a chapter in a book a higher-order task. Literate adults have simply developed the complex process of reading to such a level of proficiency that they can perform it with little effort. Such proficiency is referred to as reaching the level of automaticity (Anderson 1983; LaBerge & Samuels 1974). Many theorists agree that the vast majority of (or perhaps all) complex processes can be developed to the point of automaticity. In short, what is complex for the novice is relatively easy for the expert.

Higher-level thought, however, requires mental operations that might render even somewhat mundane tasks challenging and nonautomatic. Resnick (1987), for example, has noted that higher-level thought involves cognitive operations that render any task more controlled and more informative than it is when executed automatically. Consider the following cognitive behaviors:

- Seeking accuracy in what you do
- Being aware of your thinking at any particular time
- Operating at the edge rather than the center of your ability

Such operations as these are frequently referred to as *dispositions* because they "dispose" one to behave and think in certain ways. Use of any or all of these dispositions automatically makes a task higher order in nature. To illustrate, if you strive to seek accuracy while reading this chapter, you will automatically engage youself in a level of information processing that is more informative than that commonly used while reading. If you try to become aware of your own thinking while reading, that, too, will automatically increase the level of control involved. If you operate at the edge rather than the center of your competence while reading this chapter, you will invariably process the information much more deeply. For learning within English or the language arts classroom to be higher order, then, tasks must be engaged in from the perspective of dispositions such as these.

Principles of Learning into Pedagogy

The principles of learning outlined above specify four categories or types of thinking that should be taught and reinforced during instruction in English and the language arts: (1) contextual thinking; (2) thinking that facilitates the construction of meaning; (3) thinking that facilitates knowledge change; and (4) thinking that renders learning higher order in nature. The following chapters address these four types of thought as they apply to English and the language arts. In general, the discussion in each chapter is focused on English and language arts instruction in grades 7–12.

2 Contextual Thinking

Learning for any student within English and the language arts classrooms does not occur in a vacuum. Rather, students come to each learning situation with a set of beliefs that greatly affects their behavior. In fact, a student's experience of learning at any time is a function of her beliefs at that particular time. For example, Frank Smith (1982, 57), referring to beliefs as a theory of the world in our heads, noted the following:

> What we have in our heads is a theory of what the world is like, a theory that is the basis of all our perceptions and understanding of this world, the root of all learning, the source of all hopes and fears, motives and expectancies. And this theory is all we have. If we can make sense of the world at all, it is by interpreting our interactions with the world in light of our theory.

The importance of beliefs relative to our perception of the world implies both a deterministic and agential perspective of human behavior. That is, if our perceptions are a function of the beliefs we bring to a given situation, then we are totally determined by those beliefs. Glasser (1981) and Powers (1973) described this perspective in depth, noting that we are continually comparing the outside world to that within (our beliefs). If the outside world does not match the inside world, we act in such a way as to change the outside world (or, at least, our perception of the outside world) so that it is consistent with our internal reality. Our internal reality, then, determines how we behave. How, then, can individuals be agents of their own behavior? If human beings could not change the beliefs from which they operate, there would be little possibility of human agency. However, as Schwartz and Ogilvy (1979) pointed out, human beings have the unique ability to recognize and change the beliefs from which they operate. In fact, Bateson (1972) referred to the recognition and utilization of this uniquely human ability as the biggest bite from the tree of knowledge since the Garden of Eden. Specifically, human beings have the capability of both recognizing the attitudes and beliefs from which they operate and changing them at will. Marzano and Marzano (1987, 1988) referred to this phenomenon as changing the context from which one operates. The ultimate thinking skill, then, is the ability to recognize and alter the context one brings to a learning situation. This awareness and control will be referred to as contextual thought.

Helping students understand and explore their contextual thinking is new to education, especially in terms of the regular classroom.

However, current learning theory strongly supports the proposition that without attention to contextual thought, little substantial change in education can occur. Notably, in a series of studies, McCombs (1984, 1986, 1987) demonstrated that a knowledge and control of contextual thought is basic to self-agency. Likewise, much of the current literature in metacognition (Paris & Lindauer 1982; Paris, Lipson & Wixson 1983) reinforces the central role of contextual thought. Exploration of contextual thought does not mean that teachers take on the role of counselor. It does mean, however, that the learning environment is structured in such a way that inquiry into context is not incompatible with and, in fact, is fostered by inquiry into content.

Creating an Awareness of Contextual Thought

The first step in fostering contextual thought is to create the awareness that it exists. In other words, before students can alter the context from which they operate, they must first realize that it exists. This awareness can be engendered quite effectively through literature: Students can be made aware of the nature and function of contextual thought by studying the beliefs and attitudes of characters within specific literary works and the effects these beliefs and attitudes have on the behavior of the characters.

To facilitate this type of analysis, it is useful to introduce students to the concept of a "contextual frame." Humans approach each situation with a frame as unique as the situation. Specifically, a contextual frame has at least three general components: (1) an object, (2) a judgment about the object's value, and (3) a judgment as to whether the resources necessary to influence the object are available. We will consider each component in some detail.

Objects of a "contextual frame" can be events, people, places, things, and even abstractions. For example, an individual might have a contextual frame relative to the event "writing." Similarly an individual might have a contextual frame for the person "my English teacher." In fact, proponents of the semiotic extension theory assert that human beings tend to partition the world around them into distinctive persons, places, things, events, and abstractions (McNeill 1975) even when their environment does not necessarily fit into this partitioning.

Along with an object, a contextual frame contains a judgment about the value of the object. This value parameter has two dimensions: (1) important versus unimportant and (2) positive versus negative. For example, a student's frame about the object, American literature, would include a judgment as to whether it is important or unimportant relative to the individual's life. If the object is judged as unimportant or of little worth, then the learner will expend little energy relative to the object of the frame, in spite of his skills and abilities. However, if the student perceives American literature as important, he will bring his skills and abilities to the task. The second aspect of the value parameter is a judgment as to whether the object is positive or negative. Such a judgment might crucially depend upon the judgment as to the importance of the object, but the two are not in a fixed relation. For example, an individual can consider an object to be highly important yet negative—an object can be considered relevant to one's life because it is very threatening. Conversely, an object can be considered unimportant (not relevant) yet good.

When an object is judged as important and positive, the individual will be strongly motivated to engage in or approach the object. When an object is judged as important and negative, the individual will be strongly motivated to avoid the object or destroy or alter it. When an object is judged as unimportant and either positive or negative, the individual will have little motivation relative to the object. Figure 2.1 depicts the interrelationship between these two dimensions of value and motivation.

Positive

	Unimportant	Important
Positive	Little motivation relative to object	Motivation to engage in or approach the object
Negative	Little motivation relative to object	Motivation to avoid or destroy/ alter object

Negative

Fig. 2.1. Motivation and the two dimensions of value.

The final aspect of a contextual frame, the judgment as to the availability of resources necessary to influence the object, can also affect motivation. For example, even if the object of a frame is perceived as important and positive, the learner must believe that she has the necessary resources to affect or utilize the object. Resources can include personal skills, power, control, and such pragmatic necessities as time, materials, money, and so on. To illustrate, if a student perceives that

American literature is important but does not believe she has the skills or ability to learn it, she will put forth little energy and effort relative to the object. Similarly, if a student believes she has no power or control over how well she will do in American literature, she will bring little effort to the situation in spite of her ability. Finally, if a student believes she does not have the necessary time to do well in American literature, she will bring little motivation to that object.

To summarize, human beings have contextual frames for the persons, places, things, events, and abstractions they perceive within the world about them. These frames are composed of beliefs and attitudes about the value of the object as well as beliefs and attitudes about the availability of resources necessary to affect the object. These frames dictate the extent to which we are motivated relative to the persons, places, things, events, and abstractions of our world.

Students can be made aware of the nature of contextual frames by using the characters in literature and drama. To illustrate, consider the characters Ahab and Queequeg in Melville's *Moby Dick*. Each can be thought of as having a contextual frame relative to the object, the white whale. We might say that relative to the value parameter, Ahab believed the object (the whale) very important and very bad. In fact, the whale was the most important thing in his life; consequently, he was motivated to destroy the whale. He also believed that he possessed the necessary resources and abilities to affect the whale as evidenced by his relentless pursuit of it. Queequeg also felt the whale was important and negative. He, on the other hand, was motivated to avoid the whale, probably because he believed he was helpless to affect it in any significant way: He thought the whale was invincible. Each character had a different contextual frame relative to the object, the white whale; each character behaved differently toward the whale as a result.

An understanding of the nature and function of contextual thinking, then, can be fostered by having students analyze the contextual frames of specific characters in the literature they read relative to specific objects (i.e., events, abstractions, persons, places, things). In one class, for example, students analyzed the contextual frame the old man had toward the great fish in Hemingway's *The Old Man and the Sea*. Some students observed that the old man's frame actually changed during his battle to land the fish. At first, the old fisherman viewed the fish in a way that bordered on the mystic. He believed that the fish was directly tied to the lack of success in his immediate past. It was almost as though all of the fish he should have caught had merged into this one immensely powerful, immensely important entity. By the end of the battle, the fish had lost most, if not all, of its importance. Instead, the old man had shifted the focus of his attention to the battle within himself. In effect, the old man had changed the object of the frame from the fish to himself. This interpretation of *The Old Man and the Sea* illustrated to students the strong link between contextual frames and human motivation. Similarly, in another class, the importance of contextual frames was demonstrated as students analyzed Willie Loman's attitudes and beliefs toward the object, *success,* in *Death of a Salesman.*

The central purpose of analyzing the contextual thinking of literary characters should be to have students understand the construct of contextual thought along with the specific components of contextual frames. This understanding can then be applied to their own thought and behavior.

Making Students Aware of Their Own Contextual Thinking

Once students become aware of the nature and function of contextual frames, they can analyze their own frames and the effects they have on their behavior. This process is greatly facilitated by the use of self-journals. Journals, of course, have long been a classroom staple within English and the language arts (Atwell 1987; Calkins 1986; Macrorie 1984). In addition to the central role journals play in the composing process, they can be used as a vehicle for self-discovery, hence the name "self-journal." By having students use this form of record keeping, teachers can control those attitudes and beliefs that form the context for behavior. A journal kept for this purpose requires a more structured outline than a journal which is used only to help improve general writing skills.

Closely related to a dialogue journal (Staton 1980), a self-journal is a record of a student's thinking recorded for the purpose of discovering the nature and function of specific contextual frames. To illustrate, consider figure 2.2.

> 10/8
>
> The object I'm studying is essay tests. I guess they're a necessary evil—I have to take them in almost every class. I don't think I'll ever be good at them though. They're not good measures of what I know—I'm not good at essay tests because I never really learned how to write. I just don't know how to put the right words on what I want to say.

Fig. 2.2. Self-journal entries on components of a contextual frame.

In figure 2.2, a student has described the components of her contextual frame for the event (object), essay tests. Relative to this object, the student has identified beliefs about the value of the object and beliefs about her ability to affect or influence the event. The student apparently believes that essay tests are important in her life ("I have to take them in almost every class") and negative ("They are not good measures of what I know"). She also believes that she has little power over her performance on essay tests ("I don't think I'll ever be good at them").

In addition to her statement of beliefs relative to the object, the student has attempted to identify reasons or justifications for her belief ("I never really learned how to write"). This can be one of the most enlightening aspects of keeping a self-journal. Many times, our beliefs or attitudes are a product of irrational generalizations made from specific events. Specifically, Anderson (1983) noted that the human mind has a built-in "generalizer"—a mechanism which automatically associates specific events with other events related via general characteristics. For example, assume the student who wrote the journal entries in figure 2.2 had a negative experience with an essay exam on a previous occasion. According to Anderson, the student would store this specific experience in long-term memory. Over time, however, the specific experience could be generalized. That is, instead of remembering that she did poorly on one essay exam, she would generalize this to the assertion that she does poorly on *all* essay exams. It is at this general level that the original experience has become an attitude or a belief. Unfortunately, the generalizing process does not always follow a logical course. In fact, such theorists as Ellis (1977) and Meichenbaum (1977) assert that attitudes and beliefs are all too commonly irrational generalizations from specific events. A child is burned by a camp fire and grows up as an adult who is afraid of all types of open flames. A young girl observes that her mother is not good at mathematics and generalizes that she cannot be good at mathematics.

Given the power of attitudes and beliefs and the somewhat irrational nature of the generalizing process, it is useful for students to trace the reasons they give for their beliefs back to some initiating event. For example, the student who wrote the responses in figure 2.2 might find that she can trace her attitude about essay tests back to the specific incident. This tracing process can be greatly facilitated by free association writing in which students link present events with past events. In this student's case she would go back further and further in time until she could identify some probable initiating event. This type of free association writing is depicted in figure 2.3.

> 10/10
>
> Essay tests—English class ninth grade—I didn't really study—tried to bluff my way through—didn't work—elementary school—we started to have to take a lot of them—4th grade is when it really started—May—we had to take our first big essay test—I panicked—didn't even finish. Everyone else did great.

Fig. 2.3. Free association entries in self-journal.

In figure 2.3, the student has concluded that it was in a fourth-grade class that she began to doubt her ability at essay exams. This realization can be the beginning of the breakup of her ineffective contextual frame relative to essay exams. As the student begins to see the lack of sense in her present frame, she becomes open to replacing her old beliefs with new beliefs.

In addition to analyzing the reasons behind certain attitudes and beliefs within a contextual frame, students can also analyze the behaviors generated by a given contextual frame. That is, since a frame for any given situation dictates behaviors relative to that situation, it is useful to observe the specific behaviors that accompany a frame. Such observation is most valid if extended over a prolonged interval of time. For example, after selecting a frame for study (e.g., "essay tests") the student might observe her behavior relative to that frame for a two-week period. Again, these observations can be entered in the self-journal. Figure 2.4 contains an example of such entries.

> 10/13
>
> One thing I notice about how I act when I take an essay test is that I get very nervous. I start worrying about two days before I take it. As a matter of fact I start worrying as soon as the teacher assigns it. When I actually sit down to take the test I don't even really concentrate. I usually hand in the test early.

Fig. 2.4. Behavior entries in self-journal.

In this figure, the student has noted that she behaves in certain predictable ways every time she takes an essay examination ("I get very nervous . . . I hand in the test early"). This can be a very powerful realization for students; people seldom recognize that their behavior is related to their beliefs and even less commonly realize that their beliefs can generate their behaviors. For example, after studying her contextual frame for chemistry class and recording in her self-journal the behaviors she exhibited in that class, one student I personally worked with noticed for the first time that she behaved in very specific, highly negative ways in her chemistry class. In the process of studying her contextual frame, she traced the roots of her negative beliefs to a series of experiences in elementary school. Specifically, during one of her elementary school years, she had performed particularly poorly in science class. Up until that time, she had done quite well in science and had actually enjoyed it. In effect, therefore, her negative contextual frame for science started that year. This awareness prompted her to use *reframing* to experiment with changing her beliefs and her behavior relative to that class. As the next section illustrates, reframing is a powerful way of changing one's contextual frames. However, it is by first connecting specific behaviors with specific aspects of a contextual frame that the stage becomes set for taking control of one's contextual thinking and, consequently, one's behavior.

The Power of Reframing

The very aspect of contextual frames that renders them highly deterministic mechanisms also renders them powerful tools for self-determination. Specifically, since contextual frames are the filters through which events, situations, people, places, things, and abstractions are experienced, changing one's contextual frames will actually change one's experiences. This is perhaps best illustrated visually. As a metaphor for the concept of reframing a contextual frame, consider figure 2.5.

Fig. 2.5. Duck-rabbit. (Reprinted by permission of Macmillan Publishing Company. From *Philosophical Investigations,* 3rd ed., by Ludwig Wittgenstein. Copyright © 1973 by Macmillan Publishing Company. Copyright © Basil Blackwell & Mott, Ltd., 1958.)

If you look at this picture long enough, you will begin to see two images—one of a duck, one of a rabbit. Again, this is only a metaphor for changing a contextual frame,[1] but we might say that the figure illustrates that if you change your frame you change your perceptions: View the picture from the frame of a duck and you see a duck; view the picture from the frame of a rabbit and you see a rabbit.

Some theorists (Kuhn 1962; Schwartz and Ogilvy 1979; Watzlawick, Weakland & Fisch 1974) refer to consciously changing one's frame as a paradigm shift. In fact, they consider the phenomenon of paradigm shift as one of the most powerful of human actions. Paradigm shift allows human beings to view situations in a totally new light and consequentially solve problems that seemed insolvable. In other words, some problems are insolvable until the frame from which they are viewed is altered. Einstein, for example, asserted that the solutions to the problems created by nuclear energy lie outside the confines of our current thinking about nuclear energy (Seelig 1954) and that the solutions lie outside our paradigm or contextual frame for nuclear energy. Unfortunately, paradigm shifts are not achieved easily. They require a conscious effort on the part of an individual to change the beliefs that comprise a given contextual frame. Such an effort is referred to as reframing.

Reframing is the process of systematically addressing and, over time, changing the parameters of a specific contextual frame. At the outset, reframing is undertaken at the level of declaration—simply declaring or affirming new beliefs and attitudes—which assumes a different role for language than that commonly ascribed to it. The common conception of language is that it is a set of labels we use to describe our thoughts and ideas. From such a perspective, the use of language is a fairly passive act; it is a process by which we describe the experiences we have. However, the view of language as the vehicle that shapes rather than describes human experience was the basic assertion of Whorf (1956), who noted that, on a moment-by-moment basis, we use language to organize the somewhat random array of stimuli that bombard us. Similarly, Heidegger, in his landmark work *What Is Called Thinking?* (1968) described how the awareness and

[1] The process of shifting perceptions from the duck to the rabbit is technically not an example of reframing. It is more accurately an example of using two existing frames to interpret the same visual stimuli. As explained in this section, reframing involves changing an existing frame by declaring new attitudes and beliefs, systematically affirming them and controlling negative self-talk. The duck-rabbit illustration, however, dramatizes the power of a frame in affecting perceptions and the consequent power resulting from changing a frame.

subsequent utilization of the power of language to shape experience is the ultimate self-actualization skill.

Operationally, reframing means stating new parameters for a particular contextual frame—actually saying or writing new attitudes and beliefs. For example, the student who wrote the entries in the self-journal in figure 2.2 would begin to reframe her context for essay examinations by stating new attitudes and beliefs such as "I can do well on essay tests." Declarations of new beliefs can again be recorded in the self-journal. Of course, declarations are not actually attitudes and beliefs when initially generated. They are more like symbols of the attitudes and beliefs the student would like to possess.

In addition to declaring new attitudes and beliefs, the student would practice or rehearse the new beliefs when the object of the frame was encountered. In the example, whenever the student took an essay examination, she would mentally restate her newly declared beliefs. That is, she would make internal statements to herself such as "I will do well on this test. It will be a true reflection of my knowledge. I will be calm throughout the test." Of course, mental rehearsal of this type is commonly practiced by peak performers in a variety of situations (Suinn 1983). Peak performers consciously rehearse positive self-talk relative to situations at which they wish to excel.

While affirming the newly declared beliefs, the student would try to monitor any negative self-talk. Ellis (1977) and Meichenbaum (1977) noted that negative inner dialogue holds negative contextual frames in place. Over time, the process of affirming new attitudes and beliefs through monitoring and changing negative inner dialogue can totally alter a frame. As a result of this process, the chemistry student mentioned previously totally changed her experience and behavior in chemistry class. She not only began to enjoy the class but also started to excel in it academically.

The ability to be aware of and to control one's mental context at any given time is perhaps the ultimate cognitive skill. Although not commonly considered standard fare for the English or language arts classroom, the assertion here is that the control of context is fundamental to any study of content. The process of control involves becoming aware of the aspects of a specific contextual frame, recognizing the reasoning behind and behaviors associated with the frame, asserting new beliefs, and then rehearsing those beliefs while monitoring negative self-talk. Over time, this process cannot only result in significant behavior change but can also equip students with a tool that can make them agents of their behavior and their experience of life.

3 Constructing Meaning through Transactional Response

The concept that learning is a constructive process is receiving a growing amount of attention in the learning literature. Although this concept has appeared in the psychological literature since the late 1800s, it has most recently been associated with the work of Wittrock (1974) and Mayer (1984). Fundamentally, the constructivist stance is that learning is first and foremost a process of assembling meaning from incoming information. Another way of saying this is that information must be encoded by the learner. Inevitably, the encoding process includes a certain amount of subjectivity. The encoding generated by one learner might be quite different from that generated by another learner, even though both are exposed to the same stimuli.

The constructivist hypothesis is particularly relevant to the concept of response to literature and is quite compatible with much of the current thinking on the topic. As described by Probst (1988), current conceptions of literary response can be placed on a continuum. At one end are proponents of the New Criticism, who assert that meaning should be confined within the parameters of the text. According to the New Criticism, true literary response should be bounded by the meaning conveyed within the text without any elaboration or speculation by the reader. Probst noted that the pedagogy inspired by the New Criticism subordinated the reader to the text. Scholes (1982, 15) characterized the type of instructional practices inspired by New Criticism in the following way:

> Students were given poems to interpret with their titles removed, their author's names concealed, and their dates ignored. Anthologies were produced with the works ordered not by chronology but by the alphabet, with biographical information omitted or hidden in appendices, with no visible clues as to country or date of origin. In the name of improved interpretation, reading was turned into a mystery and the literature classroom into a chapel where the priestly instructor (who knows the authors, dates, titles, biographies, and general provenance of the texts) astounded the faithful with miracles of interpretation.

At the other end of the continuum are those who locate the source of meaning in the reader. For example, Bleich (1978) insisted that knowledge is made rather than found. For Bleich, all but the simplest acts of perception are in fact intellectual acts of making symbols and then interpreting them. Bleich illustrated his point by noting that even the act of observing a beautiful landscape is fundamentally an act of "interpretation." We perceive the landscape visually, but then immediately reformulate it into a subjective construct. It becomes an awe-inspiring landscape, an awesome landscape, a captivating landscape—each of which exists only in the mind of the perceiver.

Although Probst praised the "subjective" approach in that it places the students' thoughts at the center of curriculum, he noted that it is far too unstructured for most English or language arts classrooms:

> Although Bleich's critical theory and the sort of research and teaching that emerge from it may give us some insight into the student's role in his own literary experiences, they do not tell us as much as we might like about the contributions of the literature itself. More moderate critics and teachers, however much they respect the reader's perspective, might feel uncomfortable with a theory that places so much weight on the students' shoulders, especially in the secondary schools. On the one hand, such an approach is likely to appeal to students. It does, after all, grant them and their opinions a central place in the classroom, and thus might motivate them to participate. On the other hand, too many students are inclined to value their own unconsidered opinions too highly already, and teachers may fear the potential for misunderstanding the subjective approach. If students assume that the invitation to express and examine their own feelings and thoughts is, in fact, an invitation to say whatever they please without bothering to think, then the classroom could become unmanageable. (241–42)

In the middle of the continuum is the approach represented by Rosenblatt (1978) and Iser (1978), commonly referred to as the transactional approach. In very rough terms, the transactional approach posits an interaction, or "transaction," between the reader and the text. While the reader's unique perspective will greatly influence the shape the literary work takes in his mind, the work itself has the power to affect his responses, guiding him in some directions and steering him away from others. As Probst (1988) noted:

> Reading is thus neither a search for the meaning of the work, as in the New Critical approaches, nor a self-contained journey into one's own mind, as in subjective criticism, but an opportunity to explore and create. The task is not finding clues and solving problems, but realizing potential. The question becomes not so much, "What does the work mean?" as "What can we do with the work?" This can be a very productive question for literature teachers to raise, for it forces them to consider the perspective of

> their students and look on them as potentially active, thinking, creative individuals. (244)

It is the interactive or transactional perspective that best captures the tone of modern constructivist theories of learning. That is, modern constructivist theory asserts that the act of learning illuminates or sheds new light on both the content being learned and the learner. Similarly, transactional theory asserts that literary response is a "dance" between the reader and the text.

This chapter focuses on relatively specific categories of response that enable students to understand the text more fully while they gain insight into themselves as learners. It should be noted that the categories of response presented here are qualitatively different from those presented in previous works. Specifically, research efforts in literary response, such as those by Squire (1964) and Purves and Rippere (1968), have attempted to identify categories of student response from descriptions of behavior. In other words, the intent of that research was not to develop response categories that were easily applied to pedagogy. Unfortunately, the early efforts at categorizing response types that were meant to be translated into pedagogy were very general in nature. For example, the conclusions reached at the Anglo-American Seminar on the Teaching of English at Dartmouth College (Squire 1968, 11) included such powerful but broad principles as the following:

- Response is not passive but implies active involvement.
- Response includes not only immediate response but later effects.
- Overt response (verbal, etc.) may indicate very little of the inner response.

Current work, however, has been more specific. Probst (1988), for example, identified four basic types of literary response: personal, topical, interpretive, and formal. Although Probst explained in some depth how the English and language arts classroom can utilize and facilitate each of these types, he made no effort to tie the different types of response to underlying cognitive abilities. Indeed, given Probst's literary perspective, there would be no need or reason for him to do so. However, since this text is focused on classroom practices that teach and reinforce thinking, each response type discussed in this chapter relates to a specific aspect of cognition. Six such response types are described: imagery, emotions, value, induction, extension, and cognitive structuring. Each is considered from a transactional perspective—how it can inform the text and how it can inform the learner.

Imagery as Transactional Response

One of the most powerful yet least utilized tools for fostering transactional response is imagery. Although ignored within the study of information processing for years, imagery has received a great deal of attention in the last few decades, especially from proponents of the dual coding theory. According to that theory (Paivio 1969, 1971), information is processed into two primary modes: a linguistic mode and an imagery mode. The linguistic mode is semantic in nature and is expressed as linguistic propositions. As a metaphor, one might think of the linguistic mode as containing actual statements in long-term memory. The imagery mode, in contrast, is more episodic in nature and is expressed as mental pictures and physical sensations such as smell, taste, touch, kinesthetic association, and sound (Richardson 1983). Although the linguistic mode gradually becomes dominant over time, the more basic form in terms of primacy of response is imagery (Gazzaniga 1985; Gazzaniga & Le Doux 1978). That is, learners tend first to respond in the form of images and then encode those images as language (propositions).

As a tool for generating transactional response, imagery is particularly effective when reading literature. Responses experienced as images can be used to illuminate both the reader and the text. To illustrate, consider Stephen Spender's poem "My Parents Kept Me From Children Who Were Rough" in figure 3.1.

My Parents Kept Me From Children Who Were Rough
by
Stephen Spender

My parents kept me from children who were rough
Who threw words like stones and who wore torn clothes.
Their thighs showed through rags. They ran in the street.
And climbed cliffs and stripped by the country streams.

I feared more than tigers their muscles like iron
Their jerking hands and their knees tight on my arms.
I feared the salt-coarse pointing of those boys
Who copied my lisp behind me on the road.

They were lithe, they sprang out behind hedges
Like dogs to bark at my world. They threw mud
While I looked the other way, pretending to smile.
I longed to forgive them, but they never smiled.

Fig. 3.1. From *Selected Poems* by Stephen Spender. Copyright © 1964 by Stephen Spender. Copyright © 1934 and renewed 1962 by Stephen Spender. Copyright © 1942, 1946, 1947, 1949, 1955 by Stephen Spender. Reprinted by permission of Random House, Inc.

After reading this selection, students might be asked to note in detail the images elicited by the passage. One of the more interesting aspects of this activity is to compare images among various students. Invariably, the episodic images generated within a group of readers will vary greatly. It is important, however, to keep in mind that images are not limited to mental pictures. For example, for some ninth-grade students who had read Spender's poem, the passage elicited a strong sense of smell; still others had a strong sense of sound.

An analysis of the stimuli for such images usually leads students to an awareness of the role of the text in guiding and shaping their responses, as varied as they may be. When asked to identify the cues in Spender's poem that stimulated their images, most students were able to identify specific words and phrases in the text. Their awareness of these cues led to a closer analysis of the text in an effort to discern those aspects of imagery that were possibly intended by the author. Some students built a case for the assertion that Spender wanted to elicit a sense of taste, citing his use of the phrase "salt-coarse pointing." Others provided evidence for the assertion that the author wanted to elicit kinesthetic associations, citing his use of the words and phrases "knees tight on my arms" and "sprang" and "threw words."

An analysis of the differences in imagery responses led to students' awareness of the role of their background experiences in effecting their responses. For example, one student noted that Spender's poem reminded him of a time when he was pushed around by a group of boys. During the incident, the student's face was pressed into the mud. The poem therefore elicited remembrances of the smell and feel of mud.

In addition to its uses in literary response, imagery can also be a powerful tool in writing, especially during the incubation phase (Flower & Hayes 1980a, 1980b, 1981). Specifically, the key to the success of the incubation phase is the fluency and flexibility with which ideas are generated. Operationally, fluency can be conceptualized as the flow of ideas generated, whereas flexibility might be thought of as the range of ideas generated. Because of their holistic nature, images lend themselves to the generation of a large number of highly diverse ideas that still connect, one into another. Thus, an image can encompass a number of ideas in a free-flowing, continuous manner. As a tool in writing, then, imagery can be used as the first line of response. At a very practical level, during the incubation phase of writing, the writer might ask: "What images does my topic generate?" The words and phrases initially recorded by the writer can be thought of more as reminders of images relative to the topic rather than as expressions of complete thoughts. They are "place holders" to be filled in at a later date. As the writer revisits his work during successive drafts, the emphasis gradually shifts from using language as place holders for images to using language to stimulate images in the reader.

Writing, then, can be thought of as a transactional process. It is a written linguistic response to images experienced by the writer. The linguistic response initially helps the writer clarify her own thinking. As the writer begins to recognize the ideas she wishes to communicate, she can then use language as a tool to inform the reader. The process of the writer informing herself about the nature and function of her primitive images interacts with the process of the writer informing the reader.

Emotion as Transactional Response

Emotion is inexorably tied to cognition. In fact, Piaget (1954) noted that affective structures are "isomorphic with cognitive structures. There are not developments, one cognitive and the other affective, two separate functions, nor are there two kinds of objects, all objects are simultaneously cognitive and affective" (32). Affect is at the core of human response. Many initial reactions are emotionally based; it is only in retrospect that we understand the cognitions behind them. This is perhaps most true in literature: the hallmark of good literature is that it elicits emotions.

Affective response as a tool for transaction must include analysis from the perspective of the text and the learner. However, before affect can be analyzed, it must be noted. Simply stated, students must first become aware of the affective responses they have. Part of this awareness comes from putting a label on the type of emotion being experienced. Although there is no standard list of emotional responses, figure 3.2 is an aggregate list drawn from the works of Ellis (1977) and Mandler (1983).

admiration	doubt	mirth
affection	dread	misery
alarm	elation	optimism
amazement	embarrassment	outrage
anger	empathy	panic
anguish	enjoyment	passion
anxiety	envy	peace
appreciation	excitement	pessimism
apprehension	exultation	pity

Fig. 3.2. Aggregate list of terms for emotions.

(Fig. 3.2 continued)

astonishment
awe
belief
bitterness
bliss
calm
caring
caution
chagrin
cheer
comfort
compunction
concern
contempt
contentment
coziness
delight
depression
despair
desperation
disappointment
disbelief
discomfort
discontent
dislike
dismay
distress
faith
fear
fright
frustration
fun
fury
glee
gloom
gratitude
guilt
happiness
hatred
heartache
hope
hopelessness
horror
humiliation
hysteria
impulse
indignation
jealousy
joy
jubilation
letdown
levity
loneliness
love
playfulness
pleasure
rage
relief
resentment
respect
revenge
revulsion
sadness
satisfaction
scorn
shame
shock
solemnity
sorrow
strain
surprise
sympathy
tension
thrill
tribulation
trust
vengeance
woe
worry

The first step in using affect as a transactional response, then, is to become aware of and label the type of affect being experienced. To illustrate, assume students read the poem by Donni and George Betts in figure 3.3.

Students would try to label the emotions that the poem engendered. One student might note that the poem generated a sense of excitement. Another might note that the poem generated a feeling of apprehension.

Turning their attention to the text, students would then try to identify the specific aspect of the poem that triggered their emotional response. Usually this would involve a close inspection of the form and content of the text. For example, one student might note that it was the phrases "wrong choices," "something I'll regret," and "never any assurance" that generated an emotion of apprehension. Another student might turn to a less literal analysis, noting that it was the general reference to unlimited possibilities and free choice among those possibilities that made her feel excited.

The time has come for introspection.
I need to look at my life,
to find a direction.
Where am I going?
What do I want my life
to say about me?
The choices are mine.
My life will be what I make it.
There are so many directions.
The options are limitless.
I feel overwhelmed.
What if I make some wrong choices?
What if I do something I'll regret?
And yet I must remember
there is never any assurance
that life will be perfect.
But there is one thing
of which I can be certain . . .
I will always have ME.
My strength lies within,
and knowing that
is all the guarantee I will ever have
or truly need . . .

Fig. 3.3. Poem by Betts and Betts. Reprinted from *Seasons of Love* © 1987 by Donni Betts and George Betts, with permission from Celestial Arts, Berkeley, CA.

Turning from the text to themselves, students would analyze the nature of their emotional responses. Technically, emotions are specific types of physical reactions to stimuli (Mandler 1983). However, some people also interpret certain thoughts or types of thoughts as emotions; they might have a thought that something negative is going to happen, and thus conclude that they are experiencing a negative emotion. Additionally, the same thought or physical reaction might be interpreted differently across people. That is, the same chemical reaction or thought labeled as fear by one person might receive another label (concern) by another. In light of this, students might try to describe the various physical reactions and thoughts they associate with a specific emotion. For example, below are descriptions two students generated for the emotion of "lightness" generated by a poem they both had read:

> *Student A:* A feeling of lightness is a sense of well being. Like everything is going to turn out well—everything is as it should be.
>
> *Student B:* A feeling of lightness is actually a kind of light sensation in my chest.

Note that for Student A the emotion of lightness was associated more with certain types of thoughts, whereas for Student B it was associated with specific physical sensations.

At a deeper level of self-analysis students can determine the meaning they ascribe to various emotions. Blasi and Oresick (1986) stated that emotional responses are usually interpreted by people as meaningful in some way: something is good or bad, important or unimportant. For example, the student whose emotional response to the Betts and Betts poem was "apprehension" might analyze that feeling to determine what apprehension means to her. What are the consequences of feeling apprehensive? Does a feeling of apprehension necessarily mean that negative things will occur? At an even deeper level students can discuss the effects the meaning they ascribe to emotions has on their lives. While engaged in such a discussion, one student in a poetry class came to the realization that she did not have to behave in certain ways whenever she had specific emotions. That is, she began to perceive emotion as a constant companion in life, but not one that should necessarily be allowed to dictate her behaviors.

Value as Transactional Response

Closely related to affect as transactional response is value—the judgment as to whether a situation is good, bad, or neutral in terms of some underlying value we have. It should be noted that value as described here is a much broader construct than the value parameter described in contextual thinking. The value parameter described within contextual thought relates to a specific person, place, thing, event, or abstraction. Value as discussed here relates to underlying principles of behavior.

Value and affect are functionally related in that it is our values that commonly generate emotions. That is, we have a certain emotional response to a situation because we interpret our experiences relative to our values. For example, if we respond with negative emotions to the treatment of Boo in *To Kill a Mockingbird,* it is because we have an underlying value that human beings should be respected regardless of their intellectual capabilities. Paul (1984, 1987) has noted that the ability to recognize our values and the reasons behind them, and to acknowledge another system of reasoning which would yield a different value, is one of the most important intellectual skills of our time, given the complexity of our society. He refers to this as dialectic thinking. Fisher and Ury (1981) asserted that dialectic thinking is at the heart of negotiation.

To practice dialectic thinking, students can systematically work through their own values as triggered by literature, and ultimately understand (though not necessarily agree with) other systems of values. At a basic level, the process involves the following steps:

1. Acknowledge your emotional responses.
2. Identify the specific concept or statement that has triggered the response.
3. Describe the specific value underlying the emotional response.
4. Describe the reasoning or belief systems behind the value.
5. Articulate an opposing value.
6. Describe the reasoning behind that value.

This process is designed to be used in the context of an argument or conflict. For example, in the midst of a conversation, person A might assert that abortion should be legal. Person B might react quite negatively to this statement. If person B were to engage in the dialectic process, she would first acknowledge her strong emotional response, (anger), and the specific concept or statement that triggered it ("Abortion should be legal"). She would then try to determine the underlying value that triggered this response. In this case it might be a value that life should never be taken by another human being. At a much higher analytical level, she would try to discern the system of reasoning or beliefs that underlies the value. Discerning an underlying belief system is at the core of the dialectic process because systems of belief are invariably the foundation of value. In this case the individual might discover that her belief that life begins at conception is the underlying principle driving her value and consequent reaction to abortion. She would then try to articulate a value counter to her own (in this case, that abortion should not be banned) and a system of reasoning or beliefs that would logically support the value (in this case, that life does not begin at conception).

Although oversimplified in the example above, the dialectic process, according to Paul, has the power to create great personal insight and flexibility in dealing with others. As a tool for transactional response the dialectic process can be utilized with fiction or nonfiction. When used with fiction, the process of dialectic thinking is initially triggered by a student's recognition of a strong positive or negative emotional response. For example, while reading Gavin Lyall's short story "The Most Dangerous Game," a student might notice that he has a strong negative reaction—that as he reads the story he senses that something feels wrong to him. Next, the student would identify the specific event in the story that generated the reaction. In this case it would probably be the "hunting" of the protagonist. The student would then try to describe the value underlying that negative response. In this case that value might be "A human being should never be the subject of a hunt." Having identified the value, the student would then try to articulate the reasoning behind it, which might be stated by the student in the following way:

> Animals can rightly be hunted because they are lower forms of beings and can be used for the enjoyment of humans. However, human life is invaluable and should never be taken lightly or endangered for someone's amusement.

The pivot point of dialectic thinking is the identification and justification of an opposing value no matter how far removed from the one identified by the student. In this case an opposing value might be stated as "The validity of the hunt supersedes all other principles of human behavior." A system of reasoning that would support such a value might be stated as follows:

> Life is expendable, as is evidenced by the fact that hundreds of thousands of people are killed each year with little if any overall effect on the grand scheme of things. Survival of the fittest is the basic operating principle of life. A hunt as depicted in "The Most Dangerous Game" is an extension and celebration of this principle.

It is important to note that the purpose of articulating the reasoning behind the opposing value is to shed light on the initially identified value. It is when students deeply examine the logic behind another's values that they begin to more deeply understand their own. Thus, as repulsive and counter-intuitive as the opposing value might be ("The validity of the hunt supersedes all other principles of human behavior"), its analysis can shed light on the value which initially triggered the emotional response ("A human being should never be the subject of a hunt"). In fact, in a junior high school class where value as transactional response was used with "The Most Dangerous Game," students became intrigued with the reasoning behind their initial value (i.e., it is legitimate to hunt animals but not people) after they had analyzed the opposing value. Specifically, they began to see that the reverence held for human life could and should also be applied to animal life. This awareness led to a detailed discussion and inquiry about the rights of animals and the obligations of human beings to act as good stewards relative to animals. Only when the students analyzed the possible reasoning behind an opposing value did they truly begin to analyze the reasoning behind their own.

Just as fiction provides a rich arena in which to analyze value, so too does nonfiction. For example, students might use the process of dialectic thinking with essays on the ethics of the U.S. invasion of Panama in 1990 or the events in Eastern Europe during that same period. To illustrate, students might be presented with an editorial strongly in favor of (or against) the invasion of Panama. They would then try to identify their reaction to the editorial, the value underlying their reaction, and the system of beliefs underlying that value. Students with similar reactions might form cooperative groups. They would then articulate an opposing value and a possible system of beliefs underlying it. Cooperative groups might present their findings orally or in writing, along with statements of the personal awarenesses the process created.

To complete the transaction between reader and text, the students would turn their attention to the text in an effort to identify explicit statements of value in the editorial, along with statements that illustrate the author's reasoning behind his values.

Induction as Transactional Response

Induction is a basic human response. Simply stated, it is the act of inferring conclusions from specific information. For example, a student is engaged in induction when she concludes that a particular work was written during a specific era because of allusions to specific historical events. Although commonly confused with deduction, induction is quite different. Both induction and deduction involve drawing conclusions. However, whereas deductive conclusions can be proved, inductive conclusions at best represent a strong case (Klenk 1983). For the most part, deduction in formal learning situations is utilized in mathematics and science, where axioms and theorems can be used to construct proofs.

Unlike deduction, induction is utilized by learners quite frequently—probably from moment to moment. For example, a student in a literature course uses induction when he concludes that the teacher is in a bad mood because she closed the door rather hard as she walked into class and then dropped her books on the desk. Used as a tool for transactional analysis, however, induction is more structured in that specific types of conclusions are drawn using specific types of information. Although there are many types of inductive conclusions that can be drawn within transactional situations (since induction includes most types of inference), here we will deal with only one type of induction which is particularly suited to transactional response: induction of intentions.

Halliday (1975) listed seven basic intentions behind language use; Tough (1974, 1976) also listed seven categories of intentions, some of which overlap with Halliday's. Both schemes are oriented to the pragmatic function of language (e.g., using language to obtain information). Few of their categories relate to language use within literature. However, using speech act theory, Cooper (1984) identified four general classes of intentions that are particularly illustrative of language use in literature. More precisely, she noted that statements within literature can be divided into one of the following four categories:

1. *Constatives:* expressions of beliefs together with expressions of an intention that the audience form a like belief.
2. *Directives:* expressions of an attitude toward some prospective action by the audience together with an intention that the attitude be taken as a reason to act.
3. *Commissives:* expressions of intentions to act together with expressions of belief that such expressions obligate one to act.
4. *Acknowledgments:* expressions of feelings toward the audience.

Each of these types has subcategories. These are listed in figure 3.4.

Constatives:

You *assert* if you express a proposition.
You *predict* if you express a proposition about the future.
You *recount* if you express a proposition about the past.
You *describe* if you express that someone or something consists of certain features.
You *ascribe* if you express that a feature applies to someone or something.
You *inform* if you express a proposition that your audience does not yet believe.
You *confirm* if you express a proposition along with support for it.
You *concede* if you express a proposition contrary to what you would like to or previously did believe.
You *retract* if you express that you no longer believe a proposition.
You *assent* if you express belief in a proposition already under discussion.
You *dissent* if you express disbelief in a proposition already under discussion.

Fig. 3.4. Subcategories within types of intentions. Cooper, M. M. (1984). The pragmatics of form. How do writers discover what to do when? In R. Beach & L. S. Bridwell (Eds.). New directions in composition research (p. 115). Copyright © 1984 by The Guilford Press. Reprinted by permission of The Guilford Press.

(Fig. 3.4 continued)

You *dispute* if you express reason(s) not to believe a proposition already under discussion.
You *respond* if you express a proposition that has been inquired about.
You *suggest* if you express some, but insufficient, reason(s) to believe a proposition.
You *suppose* if you express that it is worth considering the consequences of a proposition.

Directives:

You *request* if you express that you desire your audience to act.
You *ask* if you express that you desire to know whether or not a proposition is true.
You *command* if you express that your authority is reason for your audience to act.
You *forbid* if you express that your authority is reason for your audience to refrain from acting.
You *permit* if you express that your audience's action is possible by virtue of your authority.
You *recommend* if you express the belief that there is good reason for your audience to act.

Commissives:

You *promise* if you express that you intend to act.
You *offer* if you express that you intend to act if and when your audience desires it.

Acknowledgments:

Apologies
Condolences
Congratulations
Greetings
Thanks

Inducing author intentions in a transactional sense involves drawing conclusions as to possible intentions of the author and then looking for evidence in the text itself. Focusing on the learner, it involves analyzing the effects of authors' efforts on themselves. To illustrate, students might be asked to read The Declaration of Independence.

As students soon discover, inducing authors' intentions is an inexact process of identifying the driving force behind the form and content of a text. It involves such detailed analysis as why specific words were selected, why certain rhetorical devices were used, and so on. This indirect approach is necessary because rarely, if ever, do authors directly state the intentions driving their discourse. Analyzing The Declaration of Independence for the intentions behind it, then, is a matter of searching for evidence that specific sections or even single sentences are examples of constatives, directives, commissives, and acknowledgments.

As a result of such in-depth analysis of The Declaration of Independence, one group of twelfth graders induced that one major intention of the authors was to *ascribe* specific, highly negative characteristics to the reigning monarch of England. The use of this type of constative is signified by the redundant use of a syntactic pattern beginning in the third paragraph.

> He has refused his Assent to Laws . . .
> He has forbidden his Governors to pass Laws of . . .
> He has refused to pass other Laws . . .
> He has called together Legislative bodies . . .
> He has dissolved Representative Houses . . .

This pattern continues for thirteen consecutive one-sentence paragraphs and leaves the reader with the strong sense that the king was an unfair, uncompromising leader. Students also found evidence that the authors of the Declaration of Independence were trying to *permit* their readers to act in ways counter to their natural inclinations to submit to rule from England. According to Cooper, an intention of permitting is a form of directive. Specifically, students felt that the first paragraph ("When in the Course of human Events, it becomes necessary for one People to dissolve the Political Bands which . . .") was intended to establish a tone of permission by alluding to the fact that the forthcoming declaration was a necessary occurrence within the events of human history. The declaration did not begin with a supportive argument for why it was necessary; rather it began with the assumption that the need for it was self-evident.

Finally, some students found evidence for the commissive intention of a *promise*. Specifically, they perceived the last paragraph of the declaration to be a promise to do whatever was necessary to effect the establishment of a free and independent United States of America. This promise was particularly evident in the line, "we mutually pledge to each other our Lives, our Fortunes, and our Sacred Honor."

To render induction of intentions transactional, students next analyzed their responses to the declaration. In effect, they reviewed their reactions to determine if reading it produced the effects intended by its authors. Their general conclusion was that it had. After reading the declaration, most students felt that the king was not just. They also felt a sense of permission to act. In fact, they concluded that the actions of the colonists were inevitable. Finally, the students sensed a strong commitment to action on the part of the signers. It was clear to them as readers that the authors of the document would back up their words with committed action. Almost all the students reported that the in-depth analysis of the declaration made them aware of the power of the word—in this case the power to create a nation.

Extension as Transactional Response

Extension involves identifying the abstract form underlying information and then applying that abstract form to another situation. The process of extension is at the heart of metaphor. Ortony (1980) noted that the terms in a metaphor are the topic and the vehicle. The topic is the principle subject to which the metaphoric term (the vehicle) is applied. Therefore, if we say that A is a B when it is not literally a B, then A would be the topic and B would be the vehicle. To illustrate, consider the metaphor *love is a rose*. Here love is the topic and rose is the vehicle. *Love* is not related to *rose* at a literal level but it can be considered related at an abstract level. This relationship is depicted in figure 3.5:

Literal Attributes of Love	Shared Abstract Attributes	Literal Attributes of Rose
an emotion		a flower
sometimes pleasant	desirable	beautiful
can be associated with unpleasant experiences	double edged	has thorns
often occurs in adolescence		comes in different colors

Fig. 3.5. Abstractions in a metaphor.

It is at the level of abstract form that the two are related. Speaking of metaphor, Ortony (361) noted the following:

> It is more than a linguistic or psychological curiosity. It is more than rhetorical flourish. It is also a means of conveying and acquiring new knowledge and of seeing things in new ways. It may well be that metaphors are closely related to insight. Anecdotal evidence for this abounds in the history of science. Newton's apple and Kekule's snakes are but two famous examples.

Extension, then, is fundamental to insight. In the study of literature, extension can be used as a way of relating seemingly different works. For example, the process of seeing that the underlying theme of "Pygmalion" is the same as that of "My Fair Lady" is one of identifying the abstract form that links both.

The process of extension is greatly facilitated if students progress from one literary work to another. After students have read a selection from literature, they can be asked to identify the underlying abstract pattern of the content. For example, after reading *The Old Man and the Sea*, students might be asked to identify the underlying abstract form. Extension is enhanced if students first identify the key literal points of the novel (e.g., old man and boy had a close relationship, old man had a spell of bad luck in his fishing, boy had faith in the old man, old man hooked a large fish, etc.). Once the key points of the novel have been established, students can then be asked to transform the key literal information into a more abstract or general form, as illustrated in figure 3.6.

Old man and boy had a close relationship.	→	Two people have a close relationship.
Old man had a spell of bad luck.	→	One of the partners experiences difficulties.
The young boy had faith in the old man.	→	The other partner is highly supportive.
The old man hooked a large fish.	→	The partner experiencing difficulty is faced with a difficult challenge that can bring him success.
The old man did not land the fish intact but still resolved a basic conflict in his life.	→	The partner does not directly meet the challenge but still works out some basic issues in his life.

Fig. 3.6. Literal and abstract patterns for *The Old Man and the Sea*.

The abstract form identified, students would then attempt to find another piece of literature or another incident to which the abstract form applies. For example, after creating the abstract pattern in figure

3.6, one student saw a connection between *The Old Man and the Sea* and a true life incident within her extended family. Specifically, the student likened the abstract form in Hemingway's novel to the relationship she had observed between her twin cousins. Both were very supportive of each other as children. When, in late adolescence, one twin contracted leukemia, her sibling determined to support her in overcoming the disease and was a constant companion at all therapy sessions. Sadly, the stricken sibling finally succumbed to the disease, but not before she had attained a noticeable and inspiring level of inner peace from her battle with the disease.

It is the linkages that students can make with literature and real (sometimes highly personal) life that make extension so powerful. To illustrate further, using the extension process with *Lord of the Flies*, one student described how the same abstract pattern in Golding's work also applied to the pupil's observations of how a street gang had formed in his neighborhood. Another student saw the abstract pattern in *Lord of the Flies* applying to Mussolini's rise to power in pre-World War II Italy. In still another class, the extension process was used as a framework for interpreting Joseph Campbell's (Campbell with Bill Moyers 1988) *The Power of Myth*. Students concluded that Campbell was using extension when he analyzed the commonalities in myth across different cultures and centuries.

Considering self as referent, extension can help students perceive underlying patterns in their own behavior. For example, in the class in which extension was applied to Campbell's work, the teacher also asked students to identify abstract patterns in their own behavior. Specifically, the teacher asked students to identify the abstract pattern of behavior underlying all situations in which they perceived themselves as successful. Although there were some differences among students, they discovered that, for the most part, success across all situations had common abstract elements. The pattern became known by students as the "pattern of success." Students then experimented with using their newly articulated pattern of success in situations in which they did not consider themselves successful.

Cognitive Structuring as Transactional Response

Thus far, the types of transactional response discussed are most commonly applied to such literary genres as poems, narratives, novels, plays, and short stories (although value, induction, and extension can certainly be used with expository content). Cognitive structuring, on the other hand, is most commonly used with expository information, particularly that type found in textbooks. As is the case when comprehending nonexpository content, when reading expository information the reader's task is to construct an internal representation of the information. Kintsch and van Dijk (1978) referred to this as the process of constructing a macrostructure—the creation of a subjective representation of the literal information or the microstructure. From a cognitive perspective, macrostructures can have a variety of components and a variety of forms. Specifically, macrostructures can contain any or all of the following components:

Facts

Facts are probably the simplest type of knowledge structure found within a macrostructure. Facts convey information about specific persons, places, things, events, and abstractions. That is, they commonly state such information as the following:

- The characteristics of a specific person (e.g., The fictitious character Robin Hood first appeared in English literature in the early 1800s).
- The location or characteristics of specific places (e.g., Denver is in the state of Colorado).
- The characteristics of a specific thing (e.g., The Empire State Building is over 100 stories high).
- The time or duration of a specific event (e.g., Construction began on the leaning tower of Pisa in 1174).
- The characteristics of a specific abstraction (e.g., Love is an emotion).

Time Sequences

These include important events which occurred between two points in time. For example, the events that occurred between President Kennedy's assassination on November 22, 1963, and his burial on November 25, 1963, are organized as a time sequence in most people's memories (i.e., their macrostructure). First, one thing happened, then another, then another.

Causal Networks

These involve events that result in a product or an effect. A causal network can be as simple as a single cause for a single effect. For example, the information that the game was lost because a player dropped the ball in the end zone can be organized as a causal network.

More commonly though, effects have complex networks of causes; one event affects another event which combines with a third event to affect a fourth. They, in turn, affect another, and so on. For example, the events leading up to the Civil War can be organized as a causal network. Similarly, processes can be organized as causal networks (e.g., the process for baking a cake).

Problem/Solutions

Such structures consist of a problem plus possible alternative solutions. For example, one might organize information about the different types of diction errors that can be made when writing an essay and the various ways to correct these errors as a problem/solutions macrostructure.

Episodes

Episodes are specific events that have (1) a setting (e.g., a particular time and place), (2) specific participants, (3) a particular duration, (4) a specific sequence of events, and (5) a particular cause and effect. For example, the events of Watergate could be structured as an episode. They occurred in a particular time and place; they involved specific participants; they lasted for a specific period of time; they involved a specific sequence of events; they were caused by specific events; and they had a specific effect on the country.

Generalizations

Generalizations are statements for which examples can be provided. For example, the statement, "U.S. presidents often come from families that have great wealth or influence," is a generalization. Examples can be provided for it.

Principles

Principles are generalizations considered to be general rules that apply to a given content. Normally, the following four types of principles (generalizations) are found in school-related declarative information:

1. *Cause/effect*. One event is caused by another. ("Tuberculosis is caused by the bacterium tubercle bacillus.")
2. *Correlational*. The change in one event is related to but does not necessarily cause change in another. ("The increase in lung cancer among women is directly proportional to the increase in the number of women who smoke.")

3. *Probability.* The probability of occurrences of one event can be linked to another event. ("The chance of giving birth to a boy during any one pregnancy is 0.52.")
4. *Axiomatic.* A universally accepted belief within a field for which examples can be provided. ("Complete sentences must have some form of end punctuation unless they are part of a compound or complex sentence.")

Some of these types of principles are similar to one or more of the types of structures mentioned previously. For example, cause/effect and correlational principles are similar to causal networks. Axiomatic principles are like generalizations. The difference is that principles are considered to be "rules" or "laws" within the content area. The cause/effect principle that "Tuberculosis is caused by the bacterium tubercule bacillus" is considered a rule within the field of medicine; however, the generalization that "U.S. presidents often come from families that have great wealth or influence" is not considered a rule within any field of study. Of course, this distinction implies that there is some subjectivity as to whether a certain statement is a principle or a generalization. A good rule of thumb is that principles fall into one of the four types mentioned above (cause/effect, correlational, probability, or axiomatic) and are held as generally accepted "truths" within a given field.

Concepts

Concepts are perhaps the most general and most diverse type of organizational structure within a content area. They are usually represented by a single word and commonly include many, if not all, of the other types. For example, the term *dictatorship* represents a concept. Under that, teacher or learner could state facts about specific dictators, causal networks about how specific dictators came to power, episodes about the lives of specific dictators, and principles about dictators. Thus, this one term, *dictatorship*, can be a general umbrella under which all the other types and structures fit. Another characteristic of concepts is that they are at a general enough level that examples can be provided for them. To illustrate, a number of examples of the concept of dictatorship could be easily provided by a learner knowledgeable about this concept.

Each of these eight different types of structure can be used to organize expository information. For example, consider figure 3.7, which is an adaptation from information in a social studies text.

Concepts of Dictatorship

The United States was not the only nation to suffer from the Great Depression. The nations of Europe also were hard hit. Moreover, many Europeans had been trying to repair the damage to their countries caused by World War I.

Because of the hardships under which they were forced to live, some Europeans were willing to listen to leaders who promised to make their nations rich and powerful again. Some of these leaders brought about total changes in their countries. Their actions also caused another world war.

Dictators rise to power. In the 1920s and 1930s new leaders formed governments in Italy, Germany, and Japan. The governments formed in these countries were *dictatorships*. In a dictatorship, the leader or leaders hold complete authority over the people they rule. The people living in a dictatorship have only those rights that their leader, the dictator, chooses to give them. Dictators alone make all the important decisions in their nations. The decisions made by the dictators of Italy, Germany, and Japan led to World War II.

Mussolini takes over in Italy. After World War I, many Italians wanted to feel pride in the strength of their country once again. Benito Mussolini, the founder and organizer of the Fascist Party, convinced the Italians that he and his party could strengthen the nation. To succeed, the Fascists had to take control of the economy, the government, and many other parts of Italian life.

In 1922, the Fascists took control of the Italian government, creating a dictatorship with Mussolini as leader. Italians who were against Mussolini or his government were either thrown into prison or were forced to leave the country.

Mussolini planned to increase Italy's power and wealth by taking over weaker nations. He turned to Africa and, in 1935, attacked Ethiopia. Within a few weeks the Italian army overran this East African country and added it to the Italian empire.

Hitler becomes dictator in Germany. After losing World War I, Germany continued to struggle with severe economic problems throughout the 1920s. These difficulties and the memory of their defeat in World War I brought many Germans to the Nazi Party. Its leader, Adolf Hitler, promised to make Germany the most powerful country in the world. In 1933 the Nazis won control of the German government. Hitler became Germany's dictator and silenced anyone who opposed him.

The people against whom Hitler directed his greatest hatred were the Jewish citizens of Germany. He unfairly blamed them for all of Germany's problems. By constantly repeating these false accusations, Hitler aroused public opinion in Germany against its Jewish citizens. Then he took away all civil rights and property of the Jews. Next, the police rounded up Jewish men, women,

> and children and sent them into *concentration camps,* or prison camps.
>
> Hitler promised the Germans that he would add to the territory of their nation. He immediately put the country to work making weapons and other war materials. The first nation he moved into was Austria, in 1938. Hitler annexed Austria, he explained, because most of its people were Germans.

Fig. 3.7. Information from a social studies text.

A learner might organize this information as a set of facts. In this case, the learner would simply select interesting points to store within her macrostructure for the content (e.g., In 1922, the Fascists took control of the Italian government . . . After losing World War I, Germany continued to struggle . . .). Picking out facts is not really organizing content. It is simply highlighting specific, sometimes highly idiosyncratic, information.

At a more robust level, a student might organize the content as one or more episodes. For example, the events that occurred in pre-World War II Germany can be organized as an episode, as can the events that occurred in pre-World War II Italy. Or the learner could organize much of the content under the single concept of *dictatorship* or the principle that when certain economic conditions prevail in a country, a dictator is likely to emerge.

Armed with a knowledge of these cognitive structures, then, students can organize expository content in subjective but explicit ways. These structures also give rise to expanded ways of graphically representing information. Specifically, the most common type of graphic representation is the web or spider (Heimlich & Pittelman, 1986). Although this is a very flexible format that could, no doubt, be used to represent all the cognitive structures described above, it is more powerful from a meaning construction sense to use different representations for different types of cognitive structures. Figure 3.8 presents a variety of ways of representing the various cognitive structures.

Facts

Topic

______________	______________	______________
______________	______________	______________
______________	______________	______________
______________	______________	______________
______________	______________	______________
______________	______________	______________

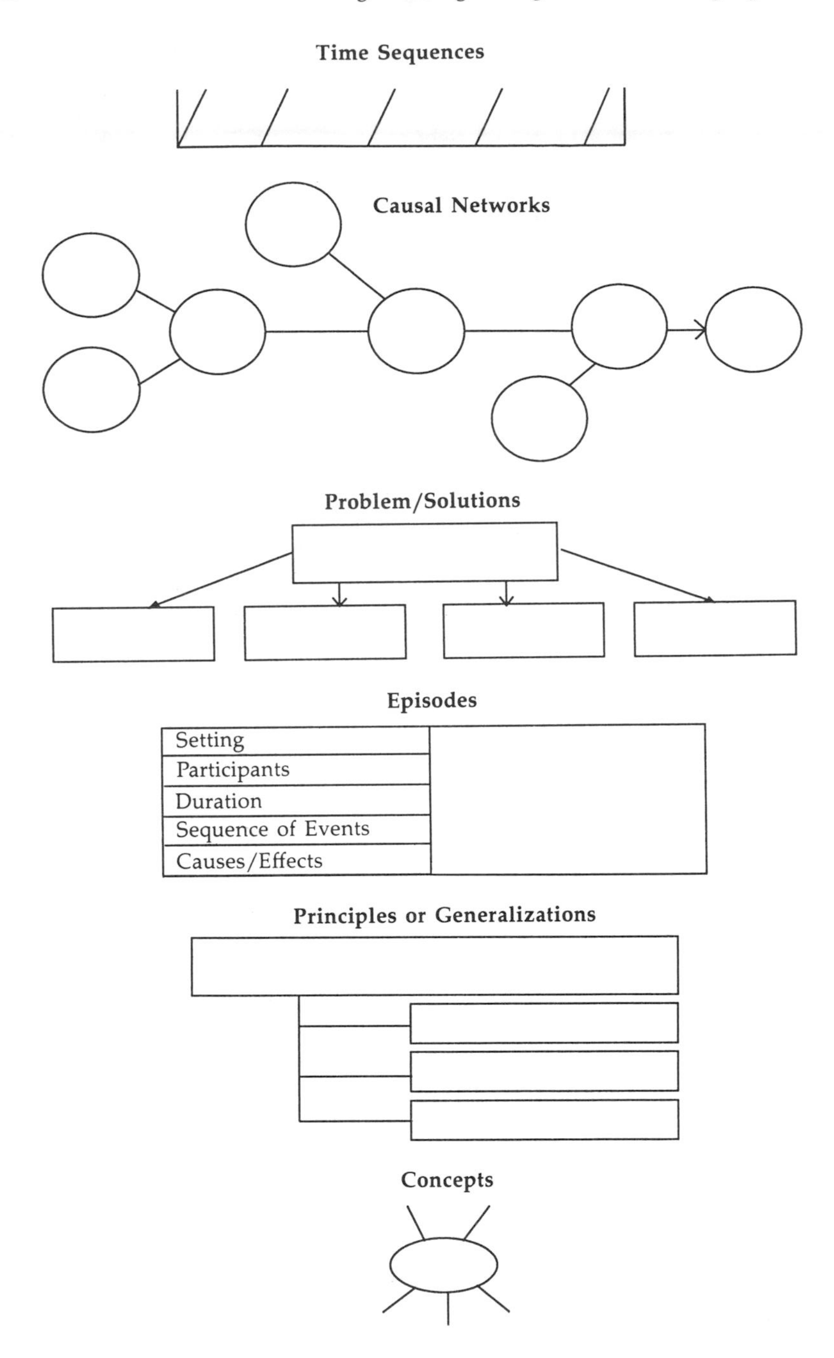

Fig. 3.8. Graphic representations for cognitive structures.

As students read expository information, they can use the various types of graphic representations to highlight the organizational structure they impose on the content. For example, a student organizing the information about Germany and Italy as a generalization might use a graphic representation like figure 3.9a. A student organizing the information under the general concept of "dictators" might use a graphic representation like figure 3.9b. Focusing on the self as referent, cognitive structuring is particularly useful in helping students understand the subjectivity involved in organizing information. After they have organized expository content, students can compare and contrast their organizations and the graphic ways they represent their organizations. As a result of this comparison, students can discuss why they chose to structure content in one way versus another. Carbo, Dunn, and Nunn (1986) asserted that the way students structure content

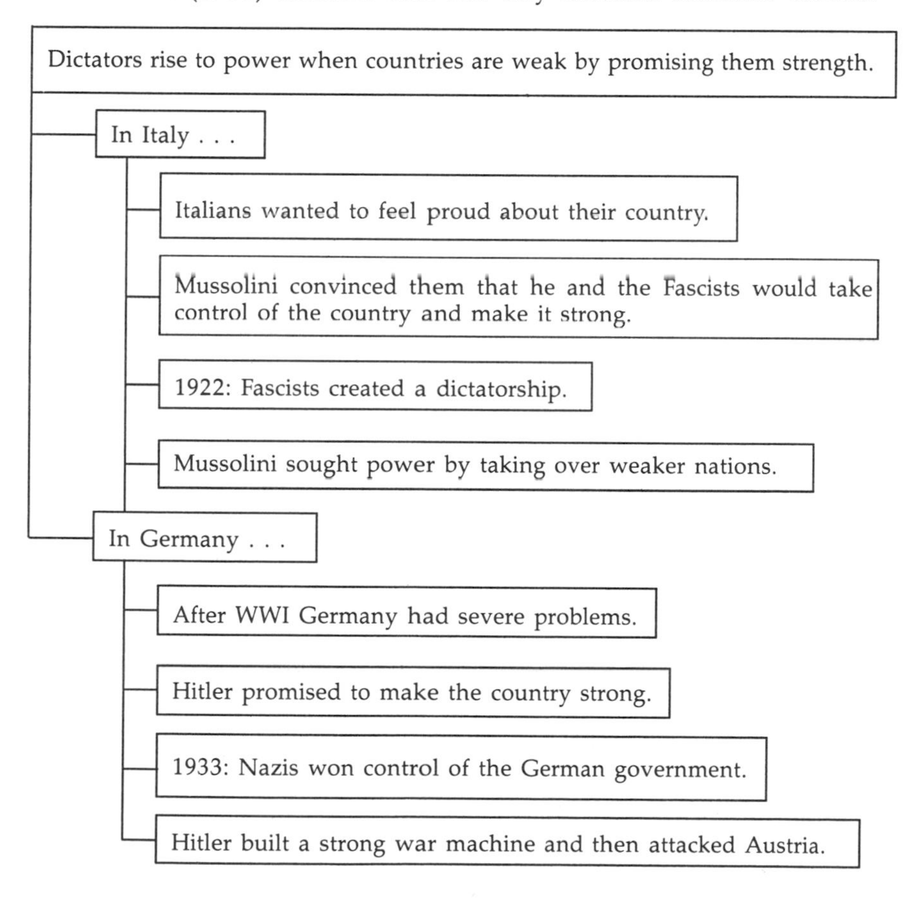

Fig. 3.9a. One way of organizing social studies information.

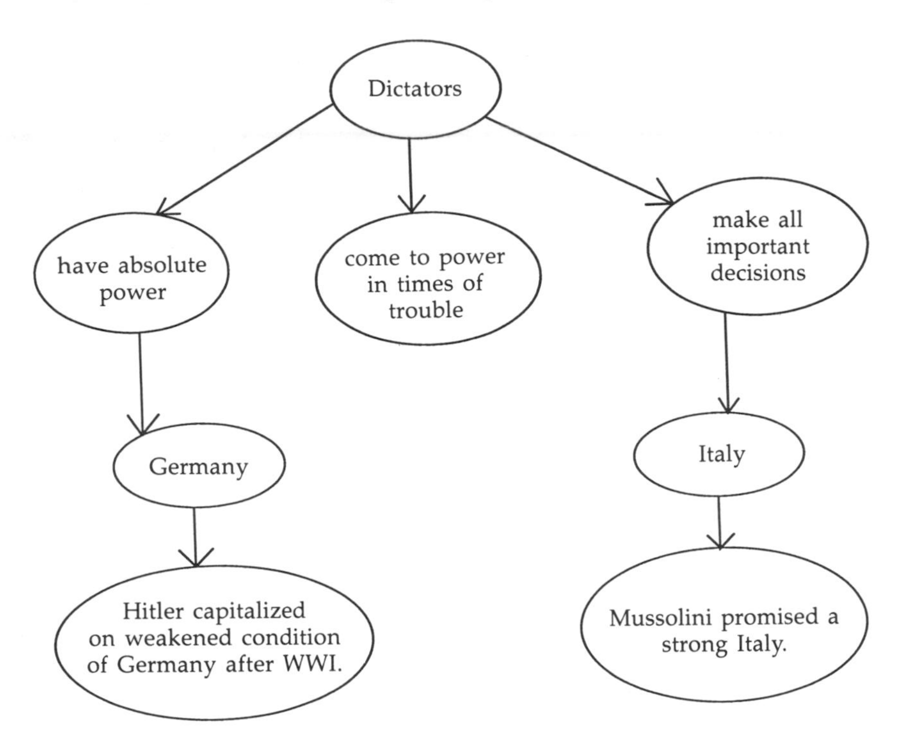

Fig. 3.9b. Another way of organizing social studies information.

provides insight into their style of learning. At the least, such analysis provides students with an awareness that they cannot assume that others (e.g., a teacher) will highlight the same information as they would when reading expository texts.

The Role of Response Journals

The six different types of transactional responses described in this chapter can produce powerful insights for students about the information they read and about themselves. A useful way of enhancing these insights is to use the double-entry response journal. Of course, double-entry journals are used extensively in reading and have been described in depth elsewhere (e.g., Atwell 1987). Briefly, double-entry journals usually contain two columns: one for student responses and one for teacher responses. However, the two columns in the double-entry journal described here are both reserved for student responses, as illustrated in figure 3.10.

11/2 The poem gave me a sense of loneliness. I think the author was trying to create this tone by the single elements he described. He would focus on one thing and describe only that. Each of his images had a single, unconnected focal point.	I think I probably look for the solitary images in the material I read or see. I guess I view myself that way, as a solitary figure.
11/5 The editorial we read on nuclear energy was very slanted. The author's intentions were obvious. He didn't give nuclear energy a chance. In fact, there wasn't one positive thing said about it. It was nothing more than a series of *assertions* and *predictions* with little to back it up.	The editorial didn't change my opinion at all. In fact, it was written so poorly that it made me become more positive about nuclear energy—the very thing he was trying to discredit.

Fig. 3.10. Double-entry journal.

In the first column of the double-entry journal the student has recorded responses to the text using the six different types discussed here: imagery, emotion, value, induction, extension, and cognitive structuring. Presumably, these responses were requested or elicited by the teacher in the form of questions or assignments (e.g., "Read the poem and respond in terms of the values it elicits in you"). In the second column the student has recorded what the transactional response has taught him about himself. This method allows for the transactional nature of the responses described in this chapter to be tracked. Thus both students and teacher can see how specific responses trigger specific insights. The response journals can be reviewed by teacher and students in a conferencing situation. Chapter 5 explores the nature and format of those conferences in depth.

4 Knowledge Development through Meaningful, Complex, Long-Term Tasks

Constructing meaning via transactional response fosters a knowledge and understanding of the content studied. However, for knowledge and understanding to grow and mature, learners must engage content in ways not commonly involved during the initial stages of learning. Specifically, the learner must engage content in meaningful, complex, long-term tasks, which are the defining characteristics of tasks that truly develop knowledge in the learner.

Meaningful Tasks

The research is fairly clear that a task is meaningful to a learner if it matches some conscious or unconscious goal or need (McCombs 1984, 1986, 1987). For example, the task of reading this book is meaningful to you if it fits a goal you have (e.g., to keep up on new formulations or new theories in English and the language arts). If the task of reading this book does not fit some personal goals (e.g., you have been assigned to read it as part of a graduate or undergraduate course that you do not care much about), then it will have little meaning for you. Additionally, the research is fairly clear that the learner must have control over a task, or its meaningfulness will be lessened (Harter 1982). For example, assuming you consider it important to read this book, you need control over the task for it to maintain its importance. If you must read the book in a one-hour sitting or can read it only ten minutes every other day due to some extenuating circumstances, you will gradually lose interest in the project.

As applied to English and language arts instruction, the principle of control implies that for knowledge to develop, students must use knowledge within tasks over which they have some control and which they can match with personal goals or needs. Of course, putting this principle into practice would effect radical changes in the classroom. Specifically, students would have opportunities to select or construct the knowledge development tasks they engage in, and would control the pace at which they progress through those tasks. The effects of such changes can be quite profound in terms of learner motivation. To illustrate, consider Atwell's (1987) comments about the effects of using Sustained Silent Reading (SSR) to enhance student self-selection relative to reading:

> I began letting my kids read their own books one day each week, and they began driving me crazy. Daily at least one student would ask, "Ms. Atwell, are we having reading today?" I didn't want to hear this. We had reading everyday—or at least that was my impression. I felt little pinpricks of conscience whenever someone voiced a desire for more SSR. But there were too many wonderful anthology selections to cover and too many activities to orchestrate. . . . (19)

Although Atwell's remarks are specific to reading, the principle of student selection and control applies to all tasks. Simply stated, if English or language arts instruction is to engage students in tasks that develop their existing knowledge, then students must not only be allowed but encouraged to construct their own tasks and have a great deal of control over their development.

Complex Tasks

Complexity here refers to cognitive complexity. According to current theory (Newmann 1989), tasks are cognitively complex if they are nonroutine and involve two or more cognitive operations that cannot be performed automatically. Nonroutine tasks are those that are not done on a frequent or systematic basis. For example, if one reads romance novels by a certain author every day, then reading romance novels by that author is a routine task.

Automaticity refers to the ability to perform a cognitive operation with little or no conscious thought. A cognitive operation is a mental process. For example, the act of writing your name is a mental process (with a physical component). Although highly complex in terms of the number and types of steps that are involved, many cognitive operations are performed with little conscious thought—they are performed at an automatic level of processing. To illustrate, reconsider writing your name: You will find that you routinely perform this mental process without ever thinking about it because it has been learned to the point of automaticity.

There are a number of cognitive operations that, by definition, are nonroutine, involve a number of cognitive operations that cannot be performed automatically, and have specific application to English and the language arts:

- Oral Inquiry
- Scientific Inquiry
- Investigatory Research
- Invention

Combining the characteristics of meaningfulness with complexity, then, one can infer that to develop their knowledge, students should select or construct tasks within English and the language arts that involve these four cognitive operations.

Long-Term Tasks

The final characteristic of knowledge development tasks is that they are long-term in nature. The extent to which a task can be long-term within the English or language arts classroom has lower and upper limits. The lower limit is two class periods, which means that a task by definition cannot be long-term in nature if it can be completed in a single class period. The upper limit, for all practical purposes, is probably a quarter, a semester, or a year, given that most English and language arts courses do not extend beyond these units. Some theorists, such as Jacques (1985), assert that for optimum knowledge development, tasks must exceed a year in duration.

Unfortunately, the principle that learning tasks should be long-term in nature flies in the face of current classroom practice. Research, in fact, indicates just the opposite—that classroom tasks are commonly short-term in nature in addition to being quite simple cognitively and under the control of the teacher (Doyle 1983; Fisher & Hiebert 1988). Regrettably, too many tasks in the English and language arts classroom are fairly simple, teacher-directed activities started and completed in a single class period. Students read a selection from an anthology or a textbook and answer questions at the end of the selection, or they complete an exercise in a composition book. If we are to take the research and theory on knowledge development seriously, then, the frequency of such tasks would be greatly diminished.

In summary, knowledge development in English and the language arts can be fostered by having students select or construct complex tasks which are long-term in nature and which involve oral inquiry, scientific inquiry, investigatory research, and invention.

Oral Inquiry

At its core, oral inquiry is the process of deeply analyzing information via structured discussion in such a way as to discover new insights. It is fundamentally Socratic in nature. Goldman (1984) noted that a Socratic inquiry involves the continual supporting and refuting of claims and counterclaims. Within oral inquiry, a claim is made. Support is then provided for the claim along with information that refutes the claim. When warranted, a counterclaim might be offered, and it, too, is held up to scrutiny by posing information that supports it and information that refutes it. During and at the conclusion of such discourse, new conclusions are drawn, old conclusions are modified or rejected.

Oral discourse, as described here, is not the norm in terms of discussions inside and outside the classroom. In fact, we rarely engage in it. To be practiced effectively, oral discourse requires certain resources and a certain structure. The major resources necessary are time and access to information because oral inquiry usually lasts for an extended period of time—two class periods, a week, two weeks, or longer. Participants also commonly find that they need more information because, more often than not during the extended process of oral inquiry, students discover that their own knowledge about the topic is highly limited.

The structure necessary for effective oral inquiry is personified by a leader whose job it is to monitor the statements being made, call for breaks when necessary to gather more information, and make observations during and at the end of the inquiry relative to both the process and the content. To illustrate, assume that a group wanted to engage in oral inquiry in an English or language arts class. They would first select a leader for the process, and then choose a topic. For illustrative purposes, assume the topic was the novelist, Ernest Hemingway. The leader's first task would be to initiate the inquiry, which might be done by asking that someone make a claim about the topic or, if none were offered, initiate a claim (e.g., "I think Hemingway was the best of the American novelists"). Other participants in the inquiry would then comment on the claim, their responses falling into three categories: (1) those that are functional relative to the inquiry, (2) those that support the claim, and (3) those that refute the claim.

Comments that are functional deal with the clarity or flow of information and include the following:

- Asking for clarification about a previous comment
- Asking for a restatement of a previous comment
- Summarizing what has been said
- Reminding the group of something that was previously said

Comments that support a claim fall into the following four categories:

- Affirming the claim, which involves agreeing with it without offering any additional information.
- Providing an argument for the claim in order to show support for it. Toulmin, Rieke, and Janik (1981) have illustrated that supportive arguments commonly include four types of comments. These are described in figure 4.1.
- Providing analogies, metaphors, and similes for the claims to help communicate the overall intent of a claim (e.g., "Hemingway was to the American novel what Babe Ruth was to baseball"). They are more persuasive than factual in nature and are meant to sway the listener or reader by virtue of their power and artistry.
- Making comparisons, which involve citing similarities and differences. Comparisons are a way of clarifying a claim. Unlike metaphors, similes, and analogies, comparisons are meant to be factual in nature (e.g., "Hemingway's style was very different from Faulkner's").

Comments that refute a claim fall into the following four major categories:

- Disagreeing, which involves the assertion that a claim is false without offering any reason or any counterclaim.
- Identifying informal fallacies, or errors of reasoning commonly made in support of a claim. Toulmin, Rieke, and Janik (1981) have identified fourteen different types of informal fallacies which are listed in figure 4.2.
- Identifying areas of ambiguity in which errors result from imprecise or inaccurate use of language. Again Toulmin, Rieke, and Janik have identified a number of such errors which are listed in figure 4.3.
- Making counterclaims which directly contradict or modify another claim (e.g., "I don't think Hemingway was the best American novelist; however, his popularity was the highest"). Additionally, counterclaims usually take an inquiry in a new direction.

1. Grounds: Once a claim is made, it is usually supported by grounds. Depending on the type of claim made, grounds may be composed of:

   - matters of common knowledge
   - expert opinion
   - previously established information
   - experimental observation
   - other information considered "factual"

   e.g., "Evidence for Hemingway's superiority can be found in reviews of his works by expert literary critic Ralph Johnson."

2. Warrants: Warrants specify or interpret the information in the grounds. That is, where grounds specify the source of support for a claim and the general nature of the support, warrants provide a detailed analysis of the information highlighted by grounds.

   e.g., "In one of Johnson's articles he notes that Hemingway's work exemplifies the first principle of good writing, namely that it should stir the emotions of the reader."

3. Backing: Backing establishes the validity of warrants. That is, warrants in and of themselves might not be wholly trusted. Consequently, it is often times appropriate for there to be some discussion of the validity or general acceptance of the warrants used.

   e.g., "The principle cited by Johnson in his critique of Hemingway is one of the most frequently cited. In fact, Pearlson notes that . . ."

4. Qualifiers: Not all warrants lead to their claims with the same degree of certainty. Consequently, qualifiers articulate the degree of certainty for the claim and/or qualifiers to the claim.

   e.g., "It should be noted that Hemingway's expertise is not appreciated by all . . ."

Fig. 4.1. Types of comments in supportive arguments.

a. Hasty generalizations. Hasty generalizations occur when someone draws conclusions from too few examples, or someone draws conclusions from an atypical example.

b. Accident. The informal fallacy of accident occurs when someone fails to recognize that an argument is based on an exception to a rule.

c. False cause. The fallacy of false cause occurs when someone confuses a temporal order of events with causality, or when someone oversimplifies a very complex causal network.

d. False analogy. False analogy occurs when someone uses an analogy for which key aspects of the two elements being compared do not match up.

e. Poisoning the well. Being committed to a position to such an extent that someone explains away everything that is offered in opposition to his or her position is referred to as "poisoning the well."

f. Begging the question (circularity). Begging the question involves making a claim and then arguing on its behalf by advancing grounds whose meaning is simply equivalent to that of the original claim.

g. Evading the issue. Evading the issue is "sidestepping" an issue by changing the topic.

h. Appealing to authority. Appealing to authority refers to invoking authority as the "last word" on an issue.

i. Arguing against the person. Rejecting a claim on the basis of derogatory facts (real or alleged) about the person making the claim is referred to as arguing against the person.

j. Arguing from ignorance. Arguing that a claim is justified simply because its opposite cannot be proved is called arguing from ignorance.

k. Appealing to the people. Appealing to the people is an attempt to justify a claim on the basis of its popularity.

l. Appealing to emotion. Using an emotion-laden or "sob" story as proof for a claim is referred to as appealing to emotion.

m. Appealing to force. Appealing to force is the use of threats as a way of establishing the validity of a claim.

n. Contradiction. The fallacy of contradiction occurs when information which is in direct opposition is presented within the same argument.

Fig. 4.2. Informal fallacies.

a. Equivocation. Equivocation is the use of words or phrases in inconsistent ways. For example, the error of equivocation would occur if an editorial asserted that protesters at a nuclear power plant were acting subdued and then later in the same editorial asserted that the protesters were loud and boisterous.

b. Amphibole. Amphibole occurs when meaning is confused because of grammatical construction.

c. Accent. The error of accent occurs when someone takes information out of context and then uses italics, boldface, or other techniques to lend false significance and meaning to a statement.

d. Composition and Division. Composition is asserting about a whole something that is true of its parts. Division is asserting about all of the parts something that is true about the whole.

Fig. 4.3. Errors of ambiguity.

To make students aware of the different types of comments that support or refute a claim, clear examples should be provided at whatever level of detail deemed necessary by the teacher and/or the students. (Students can be exposed to a select number of the different types of functional, supportive, and nonsupportive comments—warrants, backing, hasty generalizations, amphibole, etc.) Additionally, students should be provided practice in recognizing the various types of comments. For example, in one class students used the debate between Bush and Dukakis prior to the 1988 presidential election to practice recognizing the various errors listed in figures 4.2 and 4.3. To their chagrin, many students found that their favorite candidate quite frequently made many recognizable errors. Another group of students found examples of the various types of supportive and nonsupportive comments in newspaper editorials. Regardless of how students receive practice, it is imperative to the functioning of oral inquiry that students be familiar with a variety (not necessarily all) of the types of functional, supportive, and nonsupportive comments.

As an inquiry progresses, it is the leader's job to ensure that comments are fairly clear relative to their intent. She should be able to identify the general intent of a comment—identify whether it is functional in nature and provides a supportive argument, offers a metaphor, points out informal fallacies, and so on. If the purpose of a comment is not clear, the leader should challenge it and ask the originator of the comment to explain what he intended (e.g., "That last comment you made about Hemingway's work—what was your purpose? It seemed that you were providing a metaphor. Is that what you were doing?").

One of the primary functions of the inquiry leader—a function critical to a successful inquiry—is to determine when the inquiry has stalled because of lack of information. Unless participants are highly knowledgeable about the topic of the inquiry, there will come points (usually soon and often) when they simply have to stop and gather more information. A clue to the need for more information is a lack of supportive arguments being presented for claims. If participants are simply making claims and counterclaims, their discourse will by definition be fairly shallow. It will be an exchange of opinion, with little or no support provided, little or no analysis of comments taking place. Consequently, at critical points in the inquiry the leader stops the discussion and asks participants to reconvene at a set point (e.g., the next class period) after they have gathered more information. Members of the inquiry team volunteer or are appointed to collect specific information deemed necessary for further discourse.

The leader's final task is to help the group draw conclusions as a result of the inquiry. Conclusions about the topic within an inquiry fall into two basic categories: (1) awarenesses and (2) modifications and reversals. Awarenesses are new insights students have about the topic or new information generated by the inquiry. For example, relative to an oral inquiry about Hemingway, students would note any new insights they had about the author or new information gathered during their inquiry. To illustrate, as a result of a week-long inquiry about Hemingway, one group of tenth-grade students had the insight that his rearing by his prudish, highly conservative parents in Oak Park, Illinois, probably caused him to rebel and was the motivation behind his adventurous counterconventional life. They also found that *A Farewell to Arms* was highly autobiographical in nature and that Hemingway's preoccupation with war manifested itself as a theme in a number of his works.

Modifications are changes in an original position, while reversals are recognitions that original assumptions were incorrect. For example, as a result of the oral inquiry about Hemingway, a few students modified conceptions they had of the author. Some students who had initially thought Hemingway to be hedonistic and self-centered modified their perceptions as a result of discovering certain facts about his life. Specifically, the fact that Hemingway established a counterintelligence organization, called the Crook Factory, to deal with the influx of German spies in Cuba and the presence of submarines off its coast during World War II, convinced them that he was concerned for the well-being of those around him.

In addition to conclusions about the topic of the inquiry, students can draw conclusions about their behavior within the process of oral inquiry. Johnson, Johnson, Roy, and Holubec (1984) referred to this as attending to the skills of group inquiry. They listed a set of skills that includes the following:

1. Moving in and out of inquiry groups without undue noise and without bothering others
2. Staying with the inquiry by attending to what others are saying
3. Using quiet voices so that those not involved in the inquiry can work on their projects
4. Using positive social conventions such as
   a. using names
   b. looking at the speaker
   c. avoiding put-downs
   d. keeping one's hands and feet to oneself
5. Expressing support and acceptance both verbally and nonverbally through eye contact, enthusiasm, and praise
6. Encouraging others to participate

When drawing conclusions about their involvement in the oral inquiry process, individual students might note, for example, that they are not very supportive of others or that they do not utilize social conventions well.

Oral inquiry, then, always culminates in conclusions. It is a systematic way of analyzing and illuminating a topic and possibly gaining new awarenesses about oneself using oral exchange and thoughtful analysis.

Scientific Inquiry

Whereas oral inquiry focuses on clarifying through discourse, scientific inquiry focuses on explaining and predicting. Some believe scientific inquiry is at the core of knowledge development. In an edited work, Tweney, Doherty, and Mynatt (1981) chronicled the use of scientific inquiry in knowledge development within the hard sciences. Baron (1985) asserted that the scientific method is a basic way of learning. Indeed, Dewey, in *How We Think* (1933), outlined an approach to learning that is basically the process of scientific inquiry.

Although there are many models of scientific inquiry, most include the following components:

- Observing
- Analyzing
- Predicting
- Testing
- Reevaluating

For example, in a standard scientific situation an individual might first *observe* that water in a shallow pan left overnight evaporates. The individual might then *analyze* the event in an attempt to explain what happened (e.g., The water evaporated because it was exposed to the air, which was very dry). Based on this analysis the individual would *predict* what might happen under certain conditions (e.g., The lower the humidity, the quicker water evaporates). The individual would then *test* out her predictions by setting up an activity. Finally, based on the outcome of the test the individual would *reevaluate* the original analysis or explanation of what had been observed.

Unfortunately, although this scenario is quite common in the hard-science classroom, it is not common in the social sciences, let alone in the English or language arts, even though it could and should be. Specifically, within the hard sciences, the process of observing, analyzing, predicting, testing, and reevaluating is applied to physical phenomena. However, it can also be applied to psychological phenomena, where observing, analyzing, predicting, testing, and reevaluating can all be applied to human reactions. From this perspective, scientific inquiry has high utility in the English and language arts classroom since much of its content relates to human reactions. For example, the process of scientific inquiry can be used to study the effects of specific aspects of written language on readers. To illustrate, a student might become aware that she becomes easily confused by the writing of Faulkner. This represents the observational phase of scientific inquiry as it applies to psychological phenomena—noting a reaction in yourself or in others. During the analysis phase of the inquiry process the student would try to determine why she reacts unfavorably to Faulkner. She might conclude that it is Faulkner's use of long, syntactically complex sentences that is the cause of her confusion. During the prediction phase she might hypothesize that if information is written in long rather than short sentences, it will be more difficult to understand. During testing she would set up some type of activity that would test her hypothesis. She might write two short essays covering exactly the same content; however, one essay would be written with long, syntactically complex sentences, the other with short, syntactically simple sentences. These essays would then be given to selected or volunteer classmates who would each be tested on the content, perhaps in essay form. The student scientist would then evaluate the essay answers to determine which group best understood the content—the students who read the information presented with short sentences or those who read the information presented with longer sentences. Finally, during the reevaluation phase the student would reexamine her initial conclusions, either affirming or altering them based on the results of her activity. She might conclude that when sentences become too simple syntactically, the information they convey is also difficult to comprehend. Hence, information is more easily understood by the reader when the syntax used to express it is moderately complex.

Scientific inquiry, then, can apply to a variety of topics within English and language arts in that language in all its forms (e.g., poetry, oral communication, drama, signs, symbols) has some type of psychological effect on people. Topics within English and language arts that lend themselves to the process of scientific inquiry include the following:

- Determining the effects of using an improper social register in a given situation on perceptions of intelligence
- Determining the preferences of specific groups of people for specific types of genre
- Determining the effects of certain aspects of oral communication on comprehension
- Determining the effects of the use or lack of use of certain conventions within drama on audience enjoyment or understanding

Scientific inquiry as applied to English and language arts turns students into investigators of the nature and function of language.

Investigatory Research

Investigatory research is the process of filling in missing information about specific past events. To use a mundane example, when you try to discover how you caught a cold, you are involved in a simplistic form of investigatory research. At a very basic level, investigatory research is a form of problem solving since both involve filling in missing information (Rowe 1985).

Within the English or language arts classroom, investigatory research can be used to explain events that happened within literary history or within the personal lives of students. For example, one of the more interesting issues in the history of American literature is the extent to which Faulkner's Yoknapatawpha County and the events that occur there in many of his novels are autobiographical in nature. One might say that literary history is missing important information concerning the connection between Faulkner's life and the imaginary county in his works. While investigating this issue, one group of students in Charlottesville, Virginia, found that more books and scholarly articles have been written about Faulkner than about any other American novelist. Given their close proximity to Faulkner's domain, the students found themselves consulting the massive collection of Faulkner's manuscripts at the Alderman Library at the University of Virginia. They also found themselves using Joseph Blotner's abundantly detailed, two-volume, authorized biography of Faulkner, as well as more first-hand accounts of Faulkner's life by his brothers, John Faulkner and Murray C. Faulkner, along with interviews of Faulkner found in James Meriwether and Michael Millgate's edited work on Faulkner's life. In short, the process of investigatory research led students to use primary sources they probably would never have been aware of had they not engaged in the investigation.

Although investigatory research about events in literary history certainly has its place in the English and language arts classroom, the most meaningful investigations for students are related to missing information about their own pasts. Witness the incredible journey Alex Haley underwent to fill in missing information about his past while writing *Roots*. Similarly, using investigatory research, students might begin their own journey into their unknown pasts. Such a venture has the potential of generating a great deal of energy in students, given its highly personal nature. I have seen incredible energy expended by a colleague who spent five years tracing his lineage. The investigation led him to five countries and encompassed hundreds of years of family history. Now, in the best mode of oral tradition, he describes to anyone who will listen the story of his once missing past.

At the junior high level, a teacher once proudly displayed to me the products her students generated as a result of responding to the stimulus, "Identify and answer some question you have about your past." One student of Japanese ancestry decided to find out why his grandparents, who were native-born Americans, had been forced to stay in an internment camp during World War II. His investigation led him to interview his one living grandparent and to conduct a thorough analysis of the internment practices of the United States during the war. Another student decided to respond to the question, "What were my parents like as children?" His follow-up led to a thorough interview of both sets of grandparents and the collection and eventual display in written form of a series of humorous anecdotes about his parents as children.

By using investigatory research, then, students can respond to questions they have about their pasts. At the same time, their research incorporates all the aspects of the research paper; in particular, it requires them to gather information from a variety of sources. Characteristically, the information gathering involves interviewing informants and tracing primary sources such as letters and diaries. Additionally, investigatory research involves synthesizing information and making previously unmade connections. Finally, it involves presenting the newly organized information in a way that parsimoniously communicates what the student investigator has discovered.

Invention

Closely related to investigatory research is invention. The two differ in that while the core of investigatory research is the filling in of missing information, the core of invention is the creation of something new and unique. Of course, the latter is a basic characteristic of the writing process: The writer reacts to some inner need or urging and creates a story, a poem, a play. Narrative and expository forms of composing, then, within the framework of teaching and reinforcing thinking described in this book, are by definition acts of invention. Given the many fine descriptions of how the composing (invention) process can be fostered in the English and language arts classroom (e.g., Graves 1984; Murray 1985; Atwell 1987), it will not be described here. However, there are other forms of invention, not described in other works, that can also be fostered in the English and language arts classroom.

One form of invention is the creation of some new process or technique relative to language. For example, after exposing students to the traditional grammar method of diagramming sentences, one secondary English teacher challenged students to develop a method of diagrammatically representing the semantic relationships between sentences within a paragraph. The exercise led students to a study of some very sophisticated theories of discourse analysis. For example, some students investigated Turner and Greene's (1977) propositionally based scheme. Some other students consulted Halliday and Hasan's (1976) system. Still others looked into Meyer's (1975) T-unit-based approach. At the completion of the project some students had generated systems that some linguists would probably consider improvements over the existing systems. More to the point, students became intensely interested in investigating a highly abstract and sophisticated aspect of the English language.

Another way to foster invention in the English and language arts classroom is to have students perform fairly routine tasks under the burden of constraints. For example, reciting the Gettysburg Address is a task that any junior or senior high language arts student could quite easily accomplish with practice. However, conveying the information within the address without using written or oral language is quite another matter. The constraint ("Don't use written or oral language") forces the learner into an inventive mode.

The use of constraints is the basic approach employed in the popular program for enhancing thinking, entitled *Odyssey of the Mind* (Gourley 1981). Students are given relatively simple tasks made difficult by the constraints that are imposed. For example, figure 4.4 contains examples of the types of problems that would be presented to students in the *Odyssey of the Mind* program.

- Present the Gettysburg Address in a new, artificial language. Be prepared to explain the words and any rules you have created for your language.
- Create a freestanding structure that is as tall as possible, using only playing cards and masking tape.
- Build as complex a structure as possible inside a clear plastic, two-liter container for soft drinks without cutting or altering the container in any way. Entry to the inside of the container should only be through the mouth of the plastic bottle.

Fig. 4.4. Types of problems in *Odyssey of the Mind.*

Problems such as those in figure 4.4 can be constructed within the English and language arts classroom by considering conventions or practices that are standard within language, literature, or drama and then constructing tasks in which students are not allowed to use these common conventions or processes. Consider, for example, the convention of lowering the pitch of the voice to signal the end of a complete thought and raising the pitch of the voice to signal questions while speaking. Asking students to devise an alternate method of signaling complete thoughts and questions in oral language without using pitch forces them to explore aspects of language they would otherwise never question. For example, as a result of being asked to devise an alternate method of signaling complete thoughts and questions, one group of students began a study of the nature and function of inflection in various languages. They discovered that languages are not consistent in their use of inflection. Speakers of one language signal complete thoughts by raising the voice at the end; others signal complete thoughts by making clicking noises with the tongue.

Invention, then, can take many forms other than writing within the English and language arts classroom. Students can create new awarenesses about the content by creating new practices and procedures relative to the content.

In summary, there are a number of powerful and exciting tasks that are meaningful to students, cognitively complex, long-term in nature, and which lead to the development of knowledge in English and the language arts. This chapter has described four such tasks: oral inquiry, scientific inquiry, investigatory research, and invention. These tasks should be a staple within the English and language arts classroom if student knowledge is to be fully developed.

5 Providing a Structure for Higher-Order Thinking

Even though the four types of knowledge-development tasks described in chapter 4 are cognitively complex, they do not automatically involve higher-order thought. In other words, engaging in tasks, even student-generated, cognitively complex tasks that are long term in nature, does not ensure effective learning. Learners of all ages can walk through oral inquiry, scientific inquiry, investigatory research, and invention in a haphazard, uninspired way, so for learning to be most effective, the learner must bring something to the tasks. That "something" involves specific dispositions.

Dispositions, according to Resnick (1987), are habits, ways in which tasks are approached. Certain dispositions render learning higher order in nature. In this chapter, three types or categories of higher-order dispositions will be described: (1) dispositions of self-regulation, (2) dispositions of critical thinking, and (3) dispositions of creative thinking. For higher-level learning to occur, the habit of using these dispositions must be fostered.

Dispositions of Self-Regulation

One category of mental habit that reinforces higher-level learning comprises those dispositions that render the learning process under the control of the learner. These dispositions are commonly referred to as dispositions of self-regulation. Some of them are noted below:

- Being aware of one's own thinking
- Planning
- Using available resources
- Being sensitive to feedback
- Evaluating the effectiveness of one's thinking

To illustrate, a learner might make a specific plan of action before she begins her scientific inquiry project. While engaged in the project, she might attempt to pay particular attention to the type of thinking she is engaged in as well as be sensitive to how well the project is going. She might also try to be cognizant of the resources necessary for her study, possibly changing the specifics of her study based on the availability of certain resources. Finally, when the study is completed she might evaluate the effectiveness of her actions, identifying what worked and what did not work in her actions.

Dispositions of Critical Thinking

Another set of higher-level learning dispositions renders learning more critical in nature (Ennis 1985). A few of these dispositions are listed here:

- Being accurate and seeking accuracy
- Being clear and seeking clarity
- Avoiding impulsivity
- Taking a position and defending it
- Being sensitive to the level of knowledge and the feelings of others
- Being open minded

While engaged in oral inquiry, for example, a student might note that he is not being very clear in his comments and consequently adjust his discourse to do so. He might pay particular attention to the accuracy of his comments, stating things as facts only when he is relatively sure they are true. If he should feel strongly about a particular issue, he might try to defend it, all the while being open to new ideas and sensitive to the feelings and knowledge base of others. Finally, while engaged in oral inquiry, he might resist impulsive reactions, making sure to think and digest what he had heard before commenting.

Dispositions of Creative Thinking

A final category of higher-level learning dispositions contains those that make learning more creative in nature (Amabile 1983; Perkins 1984). Some of these dispositions are listed below:

- Engaging intensely in tasks even when answers or solutions are not apparent
- Pushing the limits of one's knowledge and abilities
- Generating and following one's own standards of evaluation
- Generating new ways of viewing situations outside the boundaries of standard conventions

As an example, while engaged in an invention task, the learner might realize that she is "coasting" through the project. To correct for this tendency she might push herself, even going beyond the limits of her perceived ability. She might try to view the project in new and diverse ways in an attempt to break through the assumptions she has made while conceptualizing the task. Finally, she might identify her own standards of evaluation, specifying what she expected her product to be like.

Highlighting the Dispositions

The dispositions, then, are powerful cognitive habits that transform even the most mundane tasks into insight-producing learning activities. One way of reinforcing the dispositions is to remind students of them prior to, during, or after engaging in classroom tasks. In other words, make the awareness and use of the dispositions a regular part of the classroom environment. The dispositions of self-regulation can be highlighted in the following ways:

1. While students are engaged in tasks, occasionally have them stop and notice the type and quality of their thinking. A useful strategy to this end is pairing students and having one act as listener/elicitor. The task of the listener/elicitor is to get her partner to continually describe her thinking and to evaluate it. For example, if one student is reading a passage, the listener/elicitor should periodically say, "Describe what you are thinking right now." After the student describes his thinking, the listener/elicitor should ask, "How is that helping you understand what you are reading? What else could you do to help you understand?" The reader would then continue for a minute or two (while the listener/elicitor silently reads along) until the listener/elicitor again requests a description and evaluation. After a while, the reader and listener/elicitor should switch roles.
2. Before students begin a short-term or long-term task, have them make a plan that can be described in written or oral form. Their plans should include
   a. a description of the steps to be taken along the way;
   b. milestones that indicate success;
   c. contingency steps to be used if something goes wrong.
3. Prior to beginning a short-term or long-term task, have students identify the resources necessary to complete the task. Their lists

should include the resources needed and some description of how they will obtain them.

4. During classroom tasks, periodically ask students to determine whether they are getting closer to or further away from their stated goal. If they are getting closer to their goal, the students identify what they are doing to further their progress. If they are not getting closer to their goal, the students identify and describe what is hindering their progress.
5. After students have completed a task, ask them to identify those things they would do the same if they were performing the task again, those things they would do differently, and why.

The dispositions of critical thinking can be reinforced in the following ways:

1. While students are presenting information orally or in writing, occasionally ask them to assess the extent to which they are being accurate or seeking accuracy. Students identify those things they are sure of in terms of their accuracy and those things they are not sure of. Students then discuss how they might acquire accurate information about those things of which they are unsure.
2. While students are receiving information via listening, reading, or viewing, ask them to assess the extent to which they are seeking clarity. Students identify those points on which they are not clear, along with ways of phrasing the information to make it clearer.
3. During classroom discussion and lecture, increase the amount of wait time before calling on someone. Students should first be told that wait time provides an opportunity for them to think about their answers. Additionally, students might be asked to wait for a prescribed amount of time (e.g., five seconds) before they raise their hands to answer.
4. During classroom discussion, have students identify their positions on specific topics being covered and construct support for their positions. The various positions can then be debated as part of classroom discussion.
5. During classroom discussion, ask students to rate the extent to which they are being sensitive to the feelings of others. Students identify specific behaviors that indicate sensitivity and specific behaviors that indicate a lack of sensitivity.
6. During classroom discussion, have students periodically assess the extent to which they are being open-minded. Students identify

those ideas they have rejected without much thought, along with those things they have accepted without much thought.

The disposition of creative thinking can be fostered in the following ways:

1. Before students begin a particularly difficult task, ask them to engage intensely even when no solutions or answers are readily apparent. During the task, occasionally have students stop working and rate the extent to which they are staying engaged even when the task becomes difficult.
2. Before students engage in a project, encourage them to try to push the limits of their abilities—to do things beyond what they would normally do. During the project, students occasionally stop working and rate the extent to which they are pushing themselves.
3. Before students begin a project, have them identify and write their own standards of evaluation. What specific criteria do they want their projects to meet? During the project, students occasionally stop working and assess the extent to which their projects are meeting the identified criteria.
4. Before students begin a project, ask them to brainstorm different ways of conceptualizing the task. They might identify
   a. different ways the project might look when it is completed;
   b. different ways of accomplishing the project;
   c. different applications of the final product.

Like contextual thinking, dispositional thinking can be greatly enhanced via the self-journal. For in addition to making entries in the self-journal about specific contextual frames, students can make entries relative to their observations about the dispositions of self-regulation and critical and creative thought. As a student notices his behavior relative to a specific disposition, he records his observations, thus producing a written record of his growth in awareness and use of the dispositions.

Making the reinforcement of the dispositions of self-regulation and critical and creative thought a regular part of the classroom routine will go a long way in helping students to use them. However, instilling these dispositions as habits requires a significant amount of contact between teacher and student. A useful metaphor here is that to instill the habits of self-regulation and critical and creative thought, the teacher must interact with students as a coach interacts with an athlete. As the athlete practices her sport, the coach stands by offering advice, consoling, motivating, and admonishing when necessary. Similarly, as the student engages in meaningful, complex, long-term tasks, the English teacher stands by advising, consoling, motivating, and admonishing in such ways as to reinforce the dispositions of self-regulation and critical and creative thought.

The close relationship forged between teacher and student requires a new classroom structure because the current model in which the teacher spends most of his time interacting with students as a group (even small groups) precludes the close personal involvement that characterizes a coaching relationship. One powerful structure that facilitates the coaching relationship between teacher and students is the workshop approach.

The Workshop Approach

The workshop approach is, of course, firmly established within what might be loosely termed the writing process movement. Atwell (1987), for example, has detailed the uses of the writing and reading workshops at the junior high level. What has not been well articulated, though, is how the workshop approach can be utilized for activities other than reading and writing—activities such as oral inquiry, scientific inquiry, investigatory research, and invention. Nor has it been well articulated how the workshop approach can be used to foster the dispositions of higher-level learning.

Before describing how the workshop approach can be used to these ends, we should first consider how it relates to teaching and reinforcing contextual thinking as described in chapter 2 and the transactional approach to constructing meaning as described in chapter 3. To reconcile and correlate the teaching and reinforcing of the various types of thought described in this book, it is useful to make a distinction between classes in which students are engaged in meaningful, cognitively complex, long-term tasks as described in chapter 4 versus those classes in which students are engaged in constructing meaning as described in chapter 3.

Classes in which students are engaged in constructing meaning commonly employ a traditional classroom format in which the teacher orchestrates exposure to specific aspects of the English and language arts curriculum. In such cases, transactional response as described in chapter 3 is the staple. The teacher might ask students to read a specific work of literature and then oversee specific induction activities as a method of constructing meaning in a transactional way. Or the teacher might present specific information about the concept of social register and ask students to extend the underlying pattern to other situations.

Classes in which response to content is orchestrated by the teacher are referred to as "response" classes. The working dynamic in these classes is the teacher's introducing new content that students respond to in a variety of ways, which differentiates these classes from those in which students engage in meaningful, cognitively complex, long-term tasks. The working dynamic in the latter classes is student-directed development of knowledge through in-depth exploration of content that has already been introduced. Hence, these classes are referred to as development classes. The format for development classes is the workshop approach.

Over a period of a semester, classes will alternate between sets that are response classes and sets that are development classes. For example, a possible distribution of classes over a three-week period is depicted in figure 5.1.

	M	T	W	T	F
Week #1	R	R	R	D	R
Week #2	R	D	R	D	R
Week #3	D	D	R	D	D

Fig. 5.1. Distribution of response and development classes over a three-week interval.

Thus, the English or language arts classroom geared toward improving thinking as defined in this book invokes a constant dance between response classes and development classes—between responding to English and language arts content and developing it through meaningful, cognitively complex, long-term tasks. Within both types of classes contextual thought and the dispositions of self-regulation and critical and creative thought are reinforced.

The Workshop Format

Generally, a workshop class will have three parts: a mini-lesson, an activity period, and a sharing period.

The Mini-Lesson

For the most part, the mini-lesson is used as a vehicle to provide input to students on their meaningful, cognitively complex, long-term tasks.

At first, input takes the form of helping students select or construct their tasks, as evidenced by the teacher who presents students with a list of optional, long-term tasks they can engage in over the next three weeks. A sample list of possible tasks for a class in the novel is presented in figure 5.2.

- Oral Inquiry: Have a series of discussions (oral inquiries) in which you clarify the concept of genre. Report on:
  - (a) the information you needed to collect
  - (b) the disagreements you had
  - (c) the new awarenesses you had
  - (d) your final conclusions
- Scientific Inquiry: Investigate the effects on the reader of disclosing the ending of a story at the beginning versus the end.
- Investigatory Research: Identify a question you would like answered about your roots. Research it and identify at least one novel that follows the same theme as your past.
- Invention: Create a way of expressing the story line within a novel without using the usual convention of chapters.

Fig. 5.2. List of possible long-term tasks.

Ideally, though, students will generate their own long-term tasks. Therefore, the teacher might spend the first few workshops helping students construct their own tasks using models provided in the mini-lesson.

Once students have selected or constructed their own long-term tasks, the mini-lesson is used to provide students with resources for their tasks. For example, the teacher might use the mini-lesson to illustrate and reinforce the various aspects of support to be used within oral inquiry, or he might use the mini-lesson to present various strategies for hypothesis testing to be used with scientific inquiry. In all cases the mini-lesson is quite short—from two to fifteen minutes.

The Activity Period

The activity period uses an extended time frame (20–45 minutes) in which students work individually, in pairs, or in small groups on their long-term projects. For example, during activity period one or two small groups of students might be involved in oral inquiries from which conclusions will be drawn. Other students might work independently on scientific inquiry projects, others on inventions, and so on. Concomitantly, the teacher works with small groups or conferences. (Conferencing is one of the most important facets of the workshop approach and is discussed in depth in a subsequent section.) Briefly, though, when conferencing, the teacher meets with individual students so that personalized attention can be provided. It is during conferencing that the coaching relationship between teacher and student is established.

Conferences are very short, lasting from two to ten minutes per student. These short intervals allow for a maximum amount of individual teacher/student contact. For example, assuming activity periods last an average of twenty-five minutes and conferences an average of five minutes, during each workshop a teacher can conference with up to five students. Assuming that there are thirty students in a class, a teacher can meet with each student every six workshops. Of course, more students can be seen in a given workshop if the amount of time for each conference is reduced and/or the amount of time for activity period is increased.

The Sharing Period

The sharing period is quite short, commonly lasting from two to five minutes. During this period of the workshop students discuss what they learned as a result of the mini-lesson and activity period; this might include new insights about the content, insights about themselves, or new strategies and techniques they have discovered. Students might describe their progress on their projects or they might share problems they are having with a project and ask for help from the group. In most cases sharing is quite informal, with the main purposes of discussion being the exchange of new awarenesses and whole-class focus on specific issues.

Record Keeping

The key to the success of the workshop approach is record keeping. Two forms of records—self-journals and response journals—have already been discussed. The workshop approach calls for two other types of records—learning logs and cumulative folders. Lest it appear that the teaching and reinforcing of thinking in the English or language arts classroom requires an overload of records, it should be noted that self-journals, response journals, and learning logs can be combined into the same physical record: students make entries in the same notebook for all three types of records. The types are kept separated by dates and content. For example, on any given day, a student would make an entry in one or maybe two of the different types of records. Each entry would be dated (date and time) and coded as to the type of record being kept (S = self-journal entry; R = response journal entry;

LL = learning log journal entry). Figure 5.3 illustrates a sample page from a student notebook in which multiple records have been kept.

12/2: 7:45 a.m. (S)

I've got to take an essay test tommorow in fourth period and I'm already worried about it. I mean I've already started to say negative things to myself. I'm going to try to change that.

12/2: 2.15 p.m. (LL)

I'm stuck in my project. I need to interview my grandparents to find out how they came over to this country but they're on vacation. I need another way to get that information.

12/4 2:30 p.m. (R)

The poem generated some strong emotions in me, particularly the part about how the author felt rejected as a child. I think this was the main intention of the author—conveying a sense of rejection. You can see this in line 7 . . .	I think I'm particularly sensitive to the theme of rejection because I felt it quite often when I was in elementary school . . .

Fig. 5.3. Student notebook with multiple entries.

Note that on a single day (12/2) the student made two entries in her notebook—one at 7:45 a.m. in the self-journal, relating to her contextual thinking that day, the other at 2:15 p.m. during English class. This latter entry related to her project. On another day, a response journal entry was made with two components—one relating to the student's response to the text, the other relating to her reflections about herself as a result of her response to the text.

As exemplified in figure 5.3, entries in the learning log are reserved for long-term projects. Here students record their progress on their projects and learnings that have occurred as a result of their projects. They might record conclusions they have drawn, new insights they have had, or they might use the log to work through problems they are encountering in their projects. These three types of records, self-journals, response journals, and learning logs, together then, become the stimulus for teacher/student interactions. They are the content around which the coaching relationship between teacher and students is developed.

Another type of record important to the workshop approach is the cumulative folder in which students keep tests they have taken, products they have completed, and works in progress. The cumulative folders are basically a repository for the physical evidence of students' work and knowledge development. The importance of physical evidence, or "artifacts," cannot be emphasized enough in terms of their relationship to the workshop approach.

The Role of Artifacts

Artifacts are products of student projects—more specifically, products of their meaningful, cognitively complex, long-term tasks. In school, the artifact most commonly required of students is a written or oral report of some kind. The benefits of written and oral reports include the ease with which they can be used for assessment. Written and oral reports allow a teacher to readily assess a student's level of knowledge of the content covered because essays provide permanent records of student thinking.

The major disadvantage of essays is that they are limited in what can be expressed through them. Because they express ideas as language, they are highly linear: Ideas must be presented one after the other, with little opportunity for nonlinear or multisensory representations. Additionally, not all students are good at expressing ideas in a linguistic mode. Consequently, some students might be misjudged on their knowledge and understanding of content because the artifacts they are asked to generate to display their knowledge (i.e., written and oral reports) do not match with their skills and/or inclinations.

The implication here is that students should be allowed to match their abilities and inclinations with the artifacts they use to express their knowledge, an idea which is consistent with Gardner's (1983) concept of multiple intelligences. Intelligence is not a single robust trait. There are many different types of intelligence, each with its own expression. Operationally, then, students should be allowed to display their knowledge through such diverse artifacts as

- writing and performing a song;
- creating and performing a dance;
- creating and demonstrating some physical product or physical model;
- painting and displaying a picture or sketch;
- creating and displaying a piece of sculpture;
- writing and performing a play;
- writing and reciting a poem;
- writing a short story;

- creating and demonstrating a process;
- producing a videotape or slide show.

The freedom to create such artifacts as these to demonstrate a knowledge of content would, no doubt, motivate many students more than would writing a report. The artifacts listed above, however, do not lend themselves to assessment as well as do written and oral reports.

One way, then, to increase the level of motivation students have for creating artifacts that illustrate the knowledge developed via their meaningful, cognitively complex, long-term tasks, and yet keep the ease of accountability afforded by written and oral products, is to combine the two. Students should be allowed, even encouraged, to create artifacts such as those above, but also required to develop some type of written or oral explanation to accompany these artifacts. For example, a student might paint and display a picture as her artifact for a scientific inquiry project dealing with some aspect of language. In addition to the picture, she would be required to construct a written or oral explanation. Hence, along with painting a picture depicting the conclusion drawn from her scientific inquiry, the student would turn in an essay or provide an explanation.

At first blush, this proposal might appear to encourage watering down the curriculum by allowing students to divert their energies to activities not closely tied to the acquisition of content knowledge. However, the opposite is probably more accurate. It is a basic tenet of human motivation that we engage in tasks that fit with our own interests and abilities (Glasser 1981). Consequently, if students are allowed to express their knowledge development in ways that are consistent with their interests and abilities, they will probably expend more energy in actually learning the content. Indeed, those programs that encourage students to create diverse, personalized artifacts to represent knowledge development have reported substantial gains in student knowledge (Torrance 1986). At an anecdotal level, one high school English teacher reported to me that allowing her students this freedom of expression seemed to increase their interest in the content geometrically.

Conferencing

For the most part, while students are engaged in their projects, the teacher is conferencing with individual students. Conferencing is at the heart of the workshop approach because it is only through one-to-one teacher/student interaction that the teacher can establish the coaching relationship that sets the foundation for all the types of learning described in this text. Given a strong coaching relationship, a teacher can guide students in their inner inquiry about contextual thought, or she can interact with the various types of responses students have had to classroom content. She can provide guidance for students in their long-term projects. Finally, she can provide support for the development of the dispositions of higher-level learning.

Given the multiple purposes of one-to-one teacher/student interaction, it is useful to differentiate at least three types of conferences. Each type serves different purposes.

The Attitudinal/Dispositional Conference

Contextual thought and the dispositions of higher-level learning both deal with basic psychological factors that affect students' involvement in and commitment to classroom activities. One type of conference should be devoted to interacting with students about these psychological factors. Such a conference can be called an attitudinal/dispositional conference.

Given that students have been introduced to the concept of contextual thought, they should have an understanding of the importance of attitudes and beliefs relative to their performance. Consequently, a dialogue about their attitudes and beliefs will not seem out of place. The content for a conference about attitudes and beliefs will come from the self-journal entries. To ensure privacy, students should be asked to volunteer information about their contextual thinking and select specific entries in their journals that they wish to discuss. Discussion, then, focuses on beliefs and attitudes for specific contextual frames. The teacher might ask a student to restate the attitudes and beliefs within a particular frame ("In your journal you've mentioned some specific attitudes and beliefs you have about American literature. Explain these attitudes and beliefs to me in a different way than you have in the journal"). The teacher might also use the attitudinal/dispositional conference to probe the reasons behind a certain set of attitudes and beliefs ("Let's see if we can trace some of the beliefs you have about American literature. Where and when do you think they started to form?"). If a student is trying to change his context for a given object, the teacher might provide feedback ("I've noticed you seem much more attentive in class. It looks like your reframing of your attitudes and beliefs about American literature is starting to pay off").

The attitudinal/dispositional conference is also used to reinforce the dispositions of self-regulation and critical and creative thinking. On the positive side, the teacher should use the conference to note any examples of their use. For example, relative to the disposition of self-regulation, if the teacher notices that a student appears to be aware of the necessary resources to accomplish a task, she should note it by comment ("Carmen, you're doing a great job of collecting all the materials you need before you begin working. Keep it up"). Relative to the dispositions of critical thinking, the teacher might acknowledge an observation that a student has made an effort to use information more accurately ("I noticed that you looked up in the encyclopedia the facts you used; that makes your thinking much more critical"). Relative to the disposition of creative thinking, the teacher might comment if a student is engaging intensely in a task even when easy situations or answers are not available ("I know that you've selected a very difficult project. You're doing a great job of hanging in there, even though it's tough going. Keep it up. It will pay off for you").

It is also important to note negative instances of the dispositions of self-regulation and critical and creative thought. For example, if a student is not exhibiting the self-regulatory disposition of planning for a complex task, the teacher should comment on it. ("Fred, you seem to be jumping right into your project without planning. Why don't you take some time and make a plan before you start"). If a student is not exhibiting the critical thinking disposition of taking a position and defending it when the situation warrants, the teacher might ask for correction ("Jane, you don't seem to be standing up for your position during oral inquiry. Why don't you try giving your side of the issue?"). Finally, if a student is not utilizing the creative thinking disposition of pushing herself beyond her limits, the teacher might comment ("Carmen, your work on your project is good so far, but what would happen if you really pushed yourself?").

Other than noting positive and negative instances of the dispositions of higher-level learning, the teacher can also help students create plans for increasing their use of specific dispositions. For example, if a student expresses an interest in improving her use of one (or more) of the creative thinking dispositions (e.g., engaging intensely in tasks even when answers or solutions are not apparent), the teacher might suggest specific situations in which the disposition will be most useful (e.g., while studying for a particularly difficult test) and specific strategies that can be used to enhance the disposition ("When you find yourself getting frustrated, stop working for a while and try to refresh yourself. When your energy picks up, then return to your studies"). After a plan of action has been established for a specific disposition, the teacher and student might then set up another attitudinal/contextual conference at a future date to consider the progress that has been made.

Ultimately, a student's success at whatever task he engages in is a function of his ability to monitor and control the contextual thinking which he brings to tasks and his awareness and use of the dispositions of self-regulation and critical and creative thought. The attitudinal/dispositional conference is thus one of the most important types of interactions the teacher can have with students.

The Content Conference

The content conference deals with students' understanding of and responses to the content presented in the English and language arts class. A key resource for this type of conference is the response section of the student journals. The teacher and student look through the response journal, revisiting past classroom activities and the student's responses to them ("On November 2, when we read the Gettysburg Address and I asked you to induce possible intentions by Lincoln, you commented in the response journal that . . ."). Within this interaction, the teacher might ask questions to better determine the student's understanding of the content and to probe various aspects of the student's responses:

- "Tell me why you think you reacted that way."
- "What led you to these conclusions?"
- "What did you learn from this experience?"
- "How would you react differently now if we did this same activity?"

As teacher and student revisit the content within their dialogue, a natural form of review occurs. Students are forced to recall and consequently rehearse the information about which they wrote in their response journals. As the teacher questions students about their responses, a deeper understanding of their own response patterns and an expanded view of content is effected.

The Project Conference

The purpose of the project conference is to provide guidance for students in their meaningful, cognitively complex, long-term projects. Key resources here are the learning log section of student notebooks and the cumulative folders. Together, teacher and student examine the progress of the student's project. The student might present problems she is having with the project which the teacher and student jointly work out. For example, the student might describe the difficulty she is having with a scientific inquiry project in setting up an experiment to test her hypothesis. The teacher would then help the student devise an appropriate experiment. Additionally, the project conference is used to provide guidance as to resources and skills necessary to complete the project. The teacher might point the student to a particular book or person who can help her with the next phase of the project. Within the framework of the project conference, teacher and student become partners in pursuit of a shared goal.

The Role of Reciprocity

All three of the aforementioned conferences involve highly personal experiences. Within conferences, the teacher probes the student's attitudes and dispositions, responses, and projects, requiring openness on the part of the student and a good measure of personal disclosure. If openness and personal disclosure are expected of students, they should also be offered by the teacher. Specifically, it is recommended that the teacher also keep at least a self-journal and a response journal. Then, during attitudinal/dispositional conferences, the teacher can share insights about her contextual thinking ("I've noticed that every Sunday night my self-talk about going to work the next day is very negative") or about her progress in cultivating a particular disposition ("I notice that you've been trying to improve your ability to hang in there when you can't find an answer or solution. I've been working on the same disposition. Let me tell you what I've noticed . . ."). Similarly, during response conferences the teacher can display her journal entries and compare her responses with those of the student ("Why don't you read how I reacted to the poem we read last week? My reaction was very similar to yours").

This reciprocity of openness and disclosure can be the glue that holds the coaching relationship together. For example, Atwell (1987) asserts that it is reciprocity which breaks up the current ineffective learning structure in which the teacher is viewed as the presenter of information and students as the receivers of information.

The Expanded Role of Writing

As mentioned in chapter 4, narrative and expository forms of composing are, by definition, types of invention and therefore are vehicles for knowledge development. Whenever a student writes an essay about a given topic, she develops her knowledge of the topic as a result of the composing processes. Students, then, should be encouraged and required to compose on a variety of topics within the English and language arts classroom. Indeed, this is a common practice in most classes, grades 7–12. However, a growing body of research has demonstrated that composing has a broad range of forms, few of which are fostered within schools.

It was Britton et al's study in 1975, *The Development of Writing Abilities (11–18)*, that alerted attentive English and language arts educators to the fact that school-based writing is very narrow in scope. Using writing samples from British secondary schools, Britton found that most school-based writing (and, therefore, the assignments given to students) was transactional in nature as opposed to expressive or poetic. Specifically, 63.4 percent of the writing was transactional, 5.5 percent expressive, and 17.6 percent poetic. Although these three categories have been defined somewhat differently by various researchers and theorists, Durst and Newell (1989) note that, in general, transactional writing as defined by Britton is focused on processing and manipulating information and involves such tasks as summarizing, reporting, analyzing, and theorizing.[1] Expressive writing is best understood as that which corresponds to informal talk, where rules of usage are relaxed. Expressive writing is concerned with the self and the discovery of distinctions within the self. Finally, poetic writing is used to represent the writer's experience and, in turn, to represent a virtual experience for the reader. In later works (Applebee 1981, 1984; Langer & Applebee 1987; Newell & Winograd 1989), Britton's transactional category was subdivided into at least two major categories: informational and reformulative. Informational writing enhances information processing and involves a range of cognitive operations that progresses from relatively low-level functions, such as paraphrasing, to relatively high-level functions, such as in-depth analysis of a work. Reformulative writing goes far beyond the text. Here the writer generates theories based on information gleaned from analyzing the text, but then develops those theories through such cognitive processes as hypothesis testing. The result of reformulative writing is a restructured or reformulated knowledge base.

---

[1] Transactional writing is qualitatively different from the concept of transactional response described in chapter 3. Transactional response is the cognitive process of reflecting on both content and self, with one informing the other. Transactional writing is focused on content, with little, if any, emphasis on the self.

Britton's original three categories were part of a broader attempt (Britton 1970, 1978, 1984) to construct a theory of composing based on language function and the cognition behind various functions. They were a marked departure from the traditional modes of discourse (e.g., narration, description, exposition, argumentation, and poetry) which by the 1970s had devolved to static structures taught as ends in themselves rather than as active ways of exploring ideas (Durst & Newell 1989, 377).

Britton's shift from the traditional rhetorical categories was an attempt to define composition categories based on the demands of the writing task and consequently on the type of thinking involved in each task. That shift has provided great insight. Specifically, studies by Brown (1977), Butler (1983), and Rogers (1978), which examined writing from elementary, secondary, and college students, found that students preferred poetic and expressive writing to transactional, but were given little opportunity in school to write outside the transactional mode.

From the work of Britton and others, one can conclude that for writing instruction to be truly comprehensive, it must provide students with opportunities to utilize all functional categories of writing: poetic, expressive, and (if one bifurcates the transactional category) informational and reformulative. The model for teaching thinking proposed in this text is structured so as to reinforce all four types of composing. Specifically, the three types of records used in this model (i.e., the self-journal, the response journal, and the learning log), along with the types of thinking they are meant to reinforce (i.e., contextual thinking, transactional response, knowledge development, and dispositional thought), coupled with the use of artifacts, represent a system of tasks that cuts across all four types of composing. Figure 5.4 specifies how this system relates to the expressive, informational, reformulative, and poetic functions of composing.

As figure 5.4 illustrates, the self-journal (SJ) is used to reinforce contextual thinking and the dispositions of higher-level thinking. Such writing is by nature highly expressive (E). Students discover and analyze their beliefs and attitudes as well as the mental habits (dispositions) they bring to academic and nonacademic tasks. The audience for such writing is the students themselves.

The response journal (RJ) is used for the various types of transactional interactions with literature and other content. The types of composing employed within these activities are informational (I) as well as expressive (E). Response journal writing is informational in the sense

Form of Composing	Type of Thought Reinforced	Function of Composing
SJ	Contextual thinking	E
RJ	Imagery as transactional response	I & E
RJ	Emotion as transactional response	I & E
RJ	Value as transactional response	I & E
RJ	Induction as transactional response	I & E
RJ	Extension as transactional response	I & E
RJ	Cognitive Structuring as transactional response	I & E
LL & A	Oral Inquiry as knowledge development	Rf & P
LL & A	Scientific Inquiry as knowledge development	Rf & P
LL & A	Investigatory Research as knowledge development	Rf & P
LL & A	Invention as knowledge development	Rf & P
SJ	Dispositions of higher-level learning	E

Form of composing: SJ = self-journal; RJ = response journal; LL = learning log; A = artifacts

Function of composing: E = expressive; I = informational; Rf = reformulative; P = poetic

Fig. 5.4.

that students focus on processing information in the text, albeit at a highly analytic level. Additionally, response journal writing is expressive (E) in the sense that students reflect on themselves as information processors.

The learning logs (LL) and artifacts (A) used with the knowledge development activities of oral inquiry, scientific inquiry, investigatory research, and invention foster composing that is reformulative (Rf) and poetic (P), respectively. The learning logs are used as records of students' knowledge development (reformation) as they engage in these meaningful, complex, long-term tasks. Artifacts by their very nature provide students with an outlet for poetic expression. According to Durst and Newell (1989), the operating principle underlying poetic expression is the creation of an experience by the composer, which in turn creates an experience for someone else. The artifacts described previously are experiences created by students which generate experiences in others. A student writes a song to represent what she has learned about her past as a result of investigatory research and thus creates an experience for those students who hear her song—an experience that allows the hearers to understand what the composer has felt she has gone through during her investigation.

Given the close relationship between language and thought, it is no wonder that a model of English and language arts instruction that attempts to expand the types of thinking within the classroom would also expand the types of composing fostered in the classroom. Those expansions necessitate an increase in the types of records kept and products generated by students.

Conclusions

Cultivating thinking can and should be a natural outgrowth of instruction in English and the language arts. This book has described four types of thought that are particularly compatible with English and language arts content: (1) contextual thinking, (2) thinking that facilitates the construction of meaning, (3) thinking that facilitates knowledge development, and (4) thinking that renders learning higher order in nature. Gearing English and language arts instruction to these four types of thought requires significant shifts in both the form and function of instruction. However, the results more than justify the effort. The teaching and reinforcing of thinking has the potential to illuminate the English and language arts content in ways previously not experienced. Additionally, it can transform the classroom into an arena of self-discovery and exploration for students. Finally, the cultivating of thinking can provide a common basis with which teacher and student can develop and sustain a type of relationship that exceeds the limits of pedagogy, content, and convention.

Works Cited

Amabile, T. M. (1983). *The social psychology of creativity.* New York: Springer-Verlag.

Anderson, J. (1983). *The architecture of cognition.* Cambridge, MA: Harvard University Press.

Applebee, A. N. (1981). *Writing in the secondary school.* Urbana, IL: National Council of Teachers of English.

———. (1984). *Contexts for learning to write.* Norwood, NJ: Ablex.

Atwell, N. C. (1987). *In the middle.* Portsmouth, NH: Heinemann.

Baron, J. (1985). *Rationality and intelligence.* New York: Cambridge University Press.

Bateson, G. (1972). *Steps to an ecology of mind.* New York: Ballantine Books.

Bereiter, C. (1980). Development in writing. In L. W. Gregg & E. R. Steinberg (Eds.), *Cognitive processes in writing* (pp. 73–93). Hillsdale, NJ: Lawrence Erlbaum.

Bereiter, C., & Scardamalia, M. (1982). From conversation to composition: The role of instruction in a developmental process. In R. Glaser (Ed.), *Advances in instructional psychology* (vol. 2, pp. 1–64). Hillsdale, NJ: Lawrence Erlbaum.

Beyer, B. K. (1988). *Developing a thinking skills program.* Boston: Allyn & Bacon.

Blasi, A., & Oresick, R. (1986). Emotions and cognitions in self-inconsistency. In D. J. Bearison & H. Zimiles (Eds.), *Thought and emotion: Development perspectives* (pp. 147–165). Hillsdale, NJ: Lawrence Erlbaum.

Bleich, D. (1978). *Subjective criticism.* Baltimore: Johns Hopkins University Press.

Bransford, J. D., & Johnson, M. K. (1972). Contextual prerequisites for understanding: Some investigations of comprehension and recall. *Journal of Verbal Learning and Verbal Behavior, 11,* 717–726.

Britton, J. (1970). *Language and learning.* London: Penguin.

———. (1978). The functions of writing. In C. Cooper & L. Odell (Eds.), *Research on composing* (pp. 13–28). Urbana, IL: National Council of Teachers of English.

———. (1984). Viewpoints: The distinction between participant and spectator role language in research and practice. *Research in the Teaching of English, 18,* 320–331.

Britton, J., Burgess, T., Martin, N., McLeod, A., & Rosen, H. (1975). *The development of writing abilities, (11–18).* London: Macmillan.

Brown, G. (1977). *Observing children writing: The activity and the product.* (ERIC Document Reproduction Service No. ED 162 302)

Burns, M. (1986). Teaching "what to do" in arithmetic vs. teaching "what to do and why." *Educational Leadership, 43,* 34–38.

Butler, M. (1983). Levels of engagement, rhetorical choices, and patterns of differentiation in the writing of four eleventh graders. *Dissertation Abstracts International, 45,* 440-A. (University Microfilms No. 84-10, 976)

Calkins, L. M. (1986). The art of teaching writing. Portsmouth, NH: Heinemann.

Campbell, J., with Moyers, B. (1988). *The power of myth*. New York: Doubleday.

Carbo, M., Dunn, R., & Dunn, K. (1986). *Teaching students to read through their individual learning styles*. Englewood Cliffs, NJ: Prentice-Hall.

Cooper, M. M. (1984). The pragmatics of form: How do writers discover what to do when? In R. Beach & L. S. Bridwell (Eds.), *New directions in composition research* (pp. 109–126). New York: The Guilford Press.

Covington, M. V. (1983). Motivated cognitions. In S. G. Paris, G. M. Olson, & H. W. Stevenson (Eds.), *Learning and motivation in the classroom* (pp. 139–164). Hillsdale, NJ: Lawrence Erlbaum.

de Bono, E. (1985). The CoRT Thinking Program. In J. W. Segal, S. F. Chipman, & R. Glaser (Eds.), *Thinking and learning skills: Vol. 1. Relating instruction to research* (pp. 363–388). Hillsdale, NJ: Lawrence Erlbaum.

Dewey, J. (1933). *How we think: A restatement of the relation of subjective thinking to the educative process*. Boston: D.C. Heath.

Dijk, T. A. van. (1980). *Macrostructures: An interdisciplinary study of global structures in discourse, interaction, and cognition*. Hillsdale, NJ: Lawrence Erlbaum.

Doyle, W. (1983). Academic work. *Review of Educational Research, 53*, 159–199.

Durst, R. K., & Newell, G. E. (1989). The uses of function: James Britton's category system and research on writing. *Review of Educational Research, 59*, 375–394.

Ellis, A. (1977). The basic clinical theory of rational-emotive therapy. In A. Ellis & R. Grieger (Eds.), *Handbook of rational-emotive therapy*(pp. 3–34). New York: Springer.

Ennis, R. H. (1985). Goals for a critical thinking curriculum. In A. Costa (Ed.), *Developing minds: A resource book for teaching thinking* (pp. 54–57). Alexandria, VA: Association for Supervision and Curriculum Development.

Fish, S. (1980). *Is there a text in this class? The authority of interpretive communities*. Cambridge, MA: Harvard University Press.

Fisher, C. W., & Hiebert, E. F. (1988). *Characteristics of literacy learning activities in elementary schools*. Paper presented at the annual meeting of the National Reading Conference, Tucson, AZ.

Fisher, R., & Ury, W. (1981). *Getting to yes*. New York: Penguin Books.

Flower, L., & Hayes, J. R. (1980a). The cognition of discovery: Defining a rhetorical problem. *College Composition and Communication, 31*, 21–32.

Flower, L. A., & Hayes, J. R. (1980b). The dynamics of composing: Making plans and juggling constraints. In L. W. Gregg & E. R. Steinberg (Eds.), *Cognitive processing in writing* (pp. 31–50). Hillsdale, NJ: Lawrence Erlbaum.

————. (1981). A cognitive process theory of writing. *College Composition and Communication, 32*, 365–387.

Gardner, H. (1983). *Frames of mind: The theory of multiple intelligence*. New York: Basic Books.

Gazzaniga, M. S. (1985). *The social brain*. New York: Basic Books.

Gazzaniga, M. S., & Le Doux, J. E. (1978). *The integrated mind*. New York: Plenum Press.

Glaser, R. (1984). Education and thinking: The role of knowledge. *American Psychologist, 39*, 93–104.

Glasser, W. (1981). *Stations of the mind: New directions for reality therapy*. New York: Harper & Row.

Goldman, L. (1984). Warning: The Socratic method can be dangerous. *Educational Leadership, 42*, 57–62.

Gourley, T. J. (1981). Adapting the varsity sports model to nonpsychomotor gifted students. *Gifted Child Quarterly, 25*, 164–166.

Graves, D. H. (1984). *A researcher learns to write*. Portsmouth, NH: Heinemann.

Halliday, M. (1975). *Learning how to mean—Explorations in the development of language*. London: Edward Arnold.

Halliday, M., & Hasan, R. (1976). *Cohesion in English*. London: Longman.

Harter, S. (1982). A developmental perspective on some parameters of self-regulation in children. In P. Karoly & F. H. Kanfer (Eds.), *Self-management and behavior change: From theory to practice* (pp. 165–204). New York: Pergamon Press.

Heidegger, M. C. (1968). *What is called thinking?* New York: Harper & Row.

Heimlich, J. E., & Pittelman, S. D. (1986). *Semantic mapping: Classroom applications*. Newark, DE: International Reading Association.

Iser, W. (1978). *The act of reading: A theory of aesthetic response*. Baltimore: Johns Hopkins University Press.

Jacques, E. (1985). Development of intellectual capability. In F. R. Link (Ed.), *Essays on the intellect* (pp. 107–142). Alexandria, VA. Association for Supervision and Curriculum Development.

Johnson, D. W., Johnson, R. T., Roy, P., & Holubec, E. J. (1984). *Circles of learning: Cooperation in the classroom*. Alexandria, VA: Association for Supervision and Curriculum Development.

Kintsch, W. (1974). *The representation of meaning in memory*. Hillsdale, NJ: Lawrence Erlbaum.

Kintsch, W., & Dijk, T. A. van. (1978). Toward a model of text comprehension and production. *Psychological Review, 85*, 363–394.

Klenk, V. (1983). *Understanding symbolic logic*. Englewood Cliffs, NJ: Prentice-Hall.

Kuhn, T. (1962). *The structure of scientific revolutions*. Chicago: University of Chicago Press.

LaBerge, P., & Samuels, S. J. (1974). Toward a theory of automatic information processing in reading. *Cognitive Psychology, 6*, 293–323.

Langer, J. A., & Applebee, A. N. (1987). *How writing shapes thinking*. Urbana, IL: National Council of Teachers of English.

Macrorie, K. (1984). *Writing to be read*. Upper Montclair, NJ: Boynton/Cook.

Mandler, G. (1983). The nature of emotions. In J. Miller (Ed.), *States of mind* (pp. 136–153). New York, NY: Pantheon Books.

Marzano, R. J., & Marzano, J. S. (1987). *Contextual thinking: The most basic of the cognitive skills*. (Technical Report). Aurora, CO: Mid-continent Regional

Educational Laboratory. (ERIC Document Reproduction Service No. ED 286 634)

———. (1988). A cognitive model of commitment and its implications for therapy. *Psychotherapy in Private Practice, 6*(4), 69–82.

Mayer, R. E. (1984). Aids to text comprehension. *Educational Psychologist, 19,* 30–42.

McCombs, B. (1984). Processes and skills underlying intrinsic motivation to learn: Toward a definition of motivational skills training intervention. *Educational Psychologist, 19,* 197–218.

———. (1986). The role of the self-system in self-regulated learning. *Contemporary Educational Psychology, 11,* 314–332.

———. (1987, April). *Issues in the measurement by standardized tests of primary motivation variables related to self-regulated learning.* Paper presented at the annual meeting of the American Educational Research Association, Washington, DC.

McNeill, D. (1975). Semiotic extension. In R. L. Solso (Ed.), *Information processing and cognition: The Loyola Symposium* (pp. 351–380). Hillsdale, NJ: Lawrence Erlbaum.

Meichenbaum, D. (1977). *Cognitive behavior modification.* New York: Plenum Press.

Meyer, B. J. F. (1975). *The organization of prose and its effects on memory.* New York: American Elsevier.

Murray, D. M. (1985). *A writer teaches writing.* Boston: Houghton Mifflin.

Newell, G. N., & Winograd, P. (1989). The effects of writing on learning from expository text. *Written Communication, 6,* 196–217.

Newmann, F. M. (1989, December). *Higher order thinking in social studies.* Paper presented at the Conference for Complex Thinking. Alexandria, VA.

Ortony, A. (1980). Metaphor. In R. J. Spiro, B. C. Bruce, & W. F. Brewer (Eds.), *Theoretical issues in reading comprehension* (pp. 349–366). Hillsdale, NJ: Lawrence Erlbaum.

Paivio, A. (1969). Mental imagery in associative learning and memory. *Psychological Review, 76,* 241–263.

———. (1971). *Imagery and verbal processing.* New York: Holt, Rinehart & Winston.

Paris, S. G., & Lindauer, B. K. (1982). The development of cognitive skills during childhood. In B. B. Wolman & G. Stricker (Eds.), *Handbook of developmental psychology,* (pp. 333–349). Englewood Cliffs, NJ: Prentice-Hall.

Paris, S. G., Lipson, M. Y., & Wixson, K. K. (1983). Becoming a strategic reader. *Contemporary Educational Psychology, 8,* 293–316.

Paul, R. W. (1984). Critical thinking: Fundamental to education for a free society. *Educational Leadership, 42,* 4–14.

———. (1987). Critical thinking and the critical person. In *Thinking: Report on research.* Hillsdale, NJ: Lawrence Erlbaum.

Perkins, D. N. (1984). Creativity by design. *Educational Leadership, 42,* 18–25.

———. (1985). *Where is creativity?* Paper presented at the University of Iowa Second Annual Humanities Symposium, Iowa City.

Piaget, J. (1954). *The construction of reality in the child.* New York: Basic Books.

Powers, W. T. (1973). *Behavior: The control of perception.* Chicago: Aldine.

Probst, R. E. (1988). *Response and analysis: Teaching literature in junior and senior high school.* Portsmouth, NH: Heinemann.

Purves, A. C., & Rippere, V. C. (1968). *Elements of writing about a literary work: A study of responses to literature.* Champaign, IL: National Council of Teachers of English.

Resnick, L. B. (1987). *Education and learning to think.* Washington, DC: National Academy Press.

Richardson, A. (1983). Images, definitions and types. In A. A. Sheikh (Ed.), *Imagery—Current theory, research, and application* (pp. 3–42). New York: John Wiley & Sons.

Rogers, L. (1978). The composing acts of college freshman writers: A description with two case studies. *Dissertation Abstracts International, 39,* 101A. (University Microfilms No. 78-10, 235)

Rosenblatt, L. M. (1967). *Literature as exploration.* New York: Noble & Noble.

———. (1978). *The reader, the text, the poem: The transactional theory of the literary work.* Carbondale: Southern Illinois University Press.

Rowe, H. A. H. (1985). *Problem solving and intelligence.* Hillsdale, NJ: Lawrence Erlbaum.

Rumelhart, D. E. (1980). Schemata: The building blocks of cognition. In R. J. Spiro, B. C. Bruce, & W. F. Brewer (Eds.), *Theoretical issues in reading comprehension* (pp. 33–53). Hillsdale, NJ: Lawrence Erlbaum.

Rumelhart, D. E., & Norman, D. A. (1981). Accretion, tuning and restructuring: Three modes of learning. In J. W. Colton & R. Klatzky (Eds.), *Semantic factors in cognition.* Hillsdale, NJ: Lawrence Erlbaum.

Sawada, D., & Caley, M. T. (1985). Dissipative structures: New metaphors for becoming in education. *Educational Researcher, 14,* 3–19.

Scholes, R. (1982). *Semiotics and interpretation.* New Haven, CT: Yale University Press.

Schwartz, P., & Ogilvy, J. (1979). *The emergent paradigm: Changing patterns of thought and belief.* Menlo Park, CA: Values and Lifestyles Program.

Seelig, C. (1954). *Einstein's ideas and opinions.* New York: Bonanza.

Smith, F. (1982). *Understanding reading.* New York: Holt, Rinehart and Winston.

Squire, J. R. (1964). *The response of adolescents while reading four short stories.* Champaign, IL: National Council of Teachers of English.

Squire, J. R. (Ed.). (1968). *Response to literature.* Champaign, IL: National Council of Teachers of English.

Staton, J. (1980). Writing and counseling: Using a dialogue journal. *Language Arts, 57,* 514–518.

Suinn, R. M. (1983). Imagery and sports. In A. A. Sheikh (Ed.), *Imagery: Current theory, research, and application* (pp. 507–534). New York: John Wiley & Sons.

Torrance, E. P. (1986). Teaching creative and gifted learners. In M. C. Wittrock (Ed.), *Handbook of research on teaching* (3rd ed., pp. 630–647). New York: Macmillan.

Tough, J. (1974). *Talking, thinking, and growing.* New York: Schocken Books.

———. (1976). *Listening to children.* London: Schools Council Publications.

Toulmin, S., Rieke, R., & Janik, A. (1981). *An introduction to reasoning.* New York: Macmillan.

Turner, A., & Greene, E. (1977). *The construction of a propositional text base.* Boulder: Institute for the Study of Intellectual Behavior, University of Colorado at Boulder.

Tweney, R. D., Doherty, M. E., & Mynatt, C. R. (1981). *On scientific thinking.* New York: Columbia University Press.

Vosniadou, S., & Brewer, W. F. (1987). Theories of knowledge restructuring in development. *Review of Educational Research, 51,* 51–67.

Watzlawick, P., Weakland, J., & Fisch, R. (1974). *Change: Principles of problem formation and problem resolution.* New York: W. W. Norton.

Weiner, B. (1972). Attribution theory, achievement motivation and the educational process. *Review of Educational Research, 42,* 203–215.

———. (1983). Speculations regarding the role of affect in achievement-change programs guided by attributional principles. In J. M. Levine & M. C. Wang (Eds.), *Teaching and student perceptions: Implications for learning* (pp. 57–73). Hillsdale, NJ: Lawrence Erlbaum.

Whorf, B. L. (1956). *Language, thought and reality.* Cambridge, MA: MIT Press.

Wittgenstein, L. (1970). *Philosophical investigations* (3rd ed.). Translated by G. E. M. Anscombe. New York: Macmillan.

Wittrock, M. C. (1974). Learning as a generative process. *Educational Psychologist, 11,* 87–95.

Author

Robert J. Marzano is deputy director for Training and Development at the Mid-continent Regional Educational Laboratory in Aurora, Colorado. His responsibilities include developing programs and practices, to be used in K–12 classrooms, that translate current research and theory in cognition into instructional methods. During his twenty years of work in education, he has authored more than ten books and seventy articles and chapters in books on such topics as reading and writing instruction, thinking skills, school effectiveness, and restructuring.